"The writing of *Shame Lifter* . . . . eat deal. In this book, she unzippers her soul to g. . . . . e complexities of shame in her own life. She'll draw you in by the thorough way she deals with shame, its causes, and the grace, time, and understanding needed to be freed from it. You will want to give this book to many friends who are crippled by shame, for this is a gripping story of pain, hope, and God's tender healing."

Gail MacDonald
Author of *In His Everlasting Arms*

"Through her personal story, Marilyn reveals how we can play the shame game and lose—or refuse to play and win. I have known Marilyn for twenty-five years, and her life continues to challenge me. This book did it once again in a powerful and biblical way."

Sarah Eggerichs
Love and Respect Ministries

"This book will be truly life changing for many people. Marilyn shares her heart and journey in a way that draws you in and at the same time compels you to look at your own wounds. She equips her readers with many practical steps toward healing. I will encourage many of my clients to read this book to aid in their healing process."

Dr. Peter Newhouse
Family Wellness Director
Winning At Home

"From the first word until the last, I could not put *Shame Lifter* down. Marilyn's story and gentle spirit will draw you in and soothe your soul. With an understanding heart, she describes the inner struggle of shame and illustrates how it shapes our lives. She also reveals the key that can unlock shame and usher in healing and growth. Her story is powerful, her message life-changing."

Dr. Sharon Morris May
Haven of Safety Relationships
Marriage Intensives and Counselor Training

"*Shame Lifter* will lead you deep into the *truth* of knowing who you really are in God's eyes. Be prepared to shed the shame of past experiences and rise to new life through the molding power of God's Word and the mighty power of the Holy Spirit. Marilyn will show you through her own discoveries, if you will listen, the truth indeed shall set you free!"

Christina DiMari
Author of *Ocean Star*
Founder of You're Designed to Shine

"*Shame Lifter* is real yet filled with hope and love. If you or someone you know struggles with self-hatred or shame, I encourage you to read this book. You will experience a 'lightness' and delight as the love of God reaches those places that have been hidden in the darkness. I thank Marilyn Hontz for sharing herself and her struggles so candidly."

Julie Woodley
Director, Restoring the Heart Ministry
Writer/creator of *In the Wildflowers* DVD project

shame

unwanted

shame

abandoned

unworthy

shame

failure

SHAME
Lifter

*Replacing Your
Fears and Tears
with Forgiveness,
Truth, and Hope*

MARILYN HONTZ

TYNDALE HOUSE PUBLISHERS, INC.
CAROL STREAM, ILLINOIS

Visit Tyndale's exciting Web site at www.tyndale.com

TYNDALE and Tyndale's quill logo are registered trademarks of Tyndale House Publishers, Inc.

Shame Lifter: Replacing Your Fears and Tears with Forgiveness, Truth, and Hope

Designed by Beth Sparkman

Library of Congress Cataloging-in-Publication Data

Hontz, Marilyn.
    Shame lifter : replacing your fears and tears with forgiveness, truth, and hope / Marilyn Hontz.
        p. cm.
    Includes bibliographical references.
    ISBN-13: 978-1-4143-1896-7 (sc)
    ISBN-10: 1-4143-1896-0 (sc)
    1. Shame—Religious aspects—Christianity. I. Title.
    BT714.H66 2009
    248.8′6—dc22   2008038161

Printed in the United States of America

15 14 13 12 11 10 09
  7   6   5   4   3   2   1

DEDICATION

In memory of my earthly father,
Clifford Andrew Miller,
and
In honor of my heavenly Father,
Abba

A Story of Two Fathers and Shame

*"Those who look to him are radiant;
their faces are never covered with shame."*

PSALM 34:5

CONTENTS

IN GRATITUDE

I am thankful for my husband, Paul, who first encouraged me to share part of my story at a Sunday evening church service. He prayed it would help bring healing to people who not only struggled with broken relationships, but struggled within themselves as well. Thank you, Paul: "Your love has given me great joy and encouragement" (Philemon 1:7).

I am also thankful to our four married daughters, our son, sons-in-law, and grandchildren:

Christy, Adam, Jude, and Elijah Lipscomb,
Holly, Dave, Ella, Zoe, and Baby Boy Ward,
Amanda, John, and Samuel Drury,
Abby and Tom VandenBosch, and
Paul Matthew Hontz.

Christy and Amanda, I especially want to thank both of you for reading and rereading the chapters. Your insights were extremely helpful and gave me the confidence to keep writing. Holly, Abby, and Paul Matthew, thanks for your encouraging words. Just even asking, "How's the book coming, Mom?" was very heartening.

I have loving appreciation for the best in-laws I could have ever asked for, Paul and Doris Hontz. Thank you for your prayers and phone calls during this project.

Besides my family there were others cheering me on who contributed valuable insights. I am grateful to the godly, professional counselors who took time out of their busy schedules to read all or part of the manuscript: Dr. Dan B. Allender, Dr. Scott Courey, Dr. Sharon Morris May, and Dr. Peter Newhouse.

My deepest thanks goes to Kim Miller, my editor, who believed in this book and encouraged me every step of the way. On a day when things weren't going well with the book process, Kim called and prayed with me over the phone . . . what a gift. It also speaks highly of the people at Tyndale House Publishers and their desire to support people and glorify God.

How wonderfully God used friends as well to weep and rejoice with me while I wrote. These are some of my "weep and rejoice friends" who came alongside and cheered me on—and maybe didn't even realize at the time how much they ministered to me: Carol Berens, Mary De Witt, Sharon Dryfhout, Sarah Eggerichs, Sharon Fuller, Linda George, Kathleen Hart, Betty Huizenga, Elise Mulder, Jane Seaborn, Lynn Wickstra, Jan Yoshonsis, and the Central Wesleyan Church Pastor's Prayer Team and Lydia Prayer Ladies. These prayer partners shared over and over, "I'm praying for you. How's the book coming along?" Thank you!

I've realized that everyday life happenings don't just stop when you write a book. My dreamy idea of writing a book is to write in a cozy beach cottage on Lake Michigan, a place where you can listen to the waves crash on the shore and watch the seagulls swooping in and out. It's a place where there are no interruptions, no phone calls—just complete bliss and inspiration. It's a place where I would be able to hide out until the book was completed.

Instead, however, I wrote in my kitchen and peered out my large bay window every so often to see what our Michigan weather was up to while life continued to happen around me. When I began this book, our youngest daughter was in the process of healing from a broken engagement. A married daughter found out their newborn had some health concerns. Another married daughter was in the process of adoption and had the baby for five days when the birth mom changed her mind. Our eighteen-year-old son went on a five-month missions trip to help with the HIV/AIDS situation in South Africa and set up a computer lab. I was told he would be living in the "rape and murder capital of the world," but not to worry . . . their residence was in one of the city's more "secure" neighborhoods.

And then eight days before this book was due to the publisher my husband had a heart attack. No warnings, no clogged arteries, no high cholesterol, but still a heart attack—the kind that's called the "widow maker." Thankfully, the Lord spared his life. So I wrote in my kitchen, in real life. The only waves I heard were waves of events that crashed into our house and then slowly receded. This is how life is sometimes.

I have learned some things, though, about these storms of life. It doesn't matter what you happen to be doing or where you are . . . trials come. They are normal. From my husband's close brush with death, I've learned that there really is a very thin veil between earth and heaven. We are only a few short breaths away from eternity, and that fresh realization makes me want to make the most of my days. Finally, I've noticed that while God doesn't always prevent the hard stuff from occurring in our lives, looking back, I've seen and learned that He truly is there *with* you. He is your Helper through the storms of life.

Now as the book goes to print, my husband is doing well, my daughter is newly married, my grandson's health concerns are under control, my son is safely back from South Africa, my daughter and her husband have adopted a baby boy, and life goes on. . . .

Above all, I have the highest thanks and praise to my loving heavenly Father, who is there for all of us during difficult and good times.

The Seeds of Shame

Shame is a prevailing sense of worthlessness that leads to the false belief I am what I am. I cannot change. I am hopeless.

—Robert S. McGee, *The Search for Significance*

A vague feeling of uneasiness had been nagging at me all summer. I had been asked to speak at a fund-raising event for a Christian conference center, but even after I'd prepared my talk, the discomfort remained. The committee was hoping my talk would inspire people to give financially to their camp. I felt that pressure, but there was something else too.

Not only was I feeling nervous about speaking, I was already dreading how I would feel *after* I spoke. I knew that as soon as I finished, negative voices would bombard me; not from the audience; no, much worse—negative declarations from my very own self. *Why did I say that? Oh, why didn't I remember to say this? I hope the committee wasn't disappointed. They probably didn't reach their fund-raising goal because I wasn't good enough to inspire the audience to give.* I was all too familiar with these kinds of berating thoughts. They would continue long after the speaking event until I had buried myself under a pile of self-loathing verbal garbage.

Actually, this critical self-talk was nothing new. When I first started speaking to groups, I tried to explain it away as adrenaline letdown. It was true to a degree; adrenaline always goes way up when you stand before a crowd of people. It's also true that it can come crashing down afterward.

Yet I suspected something else was wrong, and I couldn't put my finger on it. I knew that even if I heard only positive feedback from the audience, the inner pain would not go away. For some reason, I didn't think I could ever measure up to what I thought an audience wanted from me. But I also wondered if I would ever measure up to whom *I* thought I should be.

The speaking event arrived on a sunny Michigan day in August. The spacious dining room was filled to capacity with women seated at round tables, each brightened by floral centerpieces taken from late summer gardens. The numerous large windows gave a panoramic view of the serene waters of Lake Michigan. A deep calmness prevailed on the surface of the big lake. It was a calmness I longed for.

Several of my friends had driven a distance to hear me speak, but even their supportive presence did not still my apprehension. After we were seated, servers set beautifully arranged salads and baskets of warm, fragrant rolls before us. I was hungry but couldn't eat. It was then I realized I was surrounded by happy, chattering women who had no clue of my inward turmoil. Outwardly I appeared confident and totally put together. Just like the lake, my surface appeared calm and peaceful.

I watched the clock as the women ate. The program was running longer than expected. *I'm going to be late getting up to speak,* I bemoaned quietly to myself. I knew the lady sitting next to me was getting ready to take off for a trip to Florida the minute I was through speaking—she had made that perfectly clear. "My husband is already waiting in the car for me," she had informed me. I felt pressure and very responsible that she be able to leave on time.

Finally I was introduced, and the emcee mentioned I would be speaking on "Learning to Listen for God throughout Your Day." As I walked to the podium I thought, *How strange: here I am talking about God's voice, yet my own thoughts seem to drown out His voice after I finish speaking at events.* I knew as soon as I was done I would internally hear these kinds of things: *Marilyn, you forgot to mention a certain illustration.* Or, *Why did you tell the audience about that?*

Even as I spoke, I kept remembering that a man was waiting in his car for his wife to get out of the luncheon so they could leave for Florida. *You'd better hurry up, Marilyn! You don't want to keep someone waiting. Don't be a bother.* I finally concluded my talk and noted that I was only a couple of minutes over the time limit. *Good,* I thought, *now that woman can get out to her car and leave for Florida.*

As I walked back from the podium to my seat and sat down, unexpected applause erupted from the women. The emcee quickly grabbed the microphone. "Thank you, Marilyn, for sharing with us today; you've given us some things to think about. It was very meaningful." I stood up again to speak with the women who lined up near my table to talk to me. One by one, the women graciously affirmed my talk. I was a bit overwhelmed, as I was not feeling comfortable or worthy of their compliments.

Something happened, however, that was forever to change the direction of my life and the way I viewed myself. The very last woman in line said, "Thank you for your teaching today. That was the best presentation on listening for God I have heard, and I've heard several messages on that subject."

I didn't know what to say. I knew I was supposed to say thank you, but it would seem too prideful if I just said that. So as I looked at the floor I said, "Thank you," and then added, "It was nothing." At that point, the woman gently took hold of my arm. Her touch immediately made me jerk up my head and look into her blue eyes.

"Did you hear what I just said?"

"Yes," I replied rather sheepishly.

"Well," she continued, "I mean my compliments when I give them. Marilyn, do you know what your response reveals to me?"

I shook my head no as I waited for her to continue.

"Your response tells me that you live with a *shame-based perspective of life*."

Shame. I don't remember anything else she said or, for that matter, what anybody else said that afternoon. The word *shame* lodged in my throat like a vitamin pill that was stuck for lack of enough water.

Shame. I thought about that word as I made the hour-long trip home.

Shame. Was it true? Did I have a shame-based perspective of life?

Driving home from that luncheon, I tried to sort through the difference between guilt and shame. Guilt, as I understood it, meant "I have done something wrong, and I feel terrible about it." I knew I had not done anything *wrong* at the speaking event, yet I still felt awful.

I then went on a deep soul-searching journey, asking God if shame existed in my life because of a breach between Him and me. *God, is there anything I need to make right with You? Did I do something wrong?* Nothing came to mind. Silence.

Hey, can't shame be a good thing? I asked myself. If used appropriately, couldn't shame reveal something that needs to be corrected? Maybe it was okay that I had this "shame-based perspective of life," whatever that meant.

At that point I didn't understand the difference between guilt and shame. I had often heard people use the two words interchangeably. Guilt nails you on what you have *done*; shame, on the other hand, hits at the core of a person—*who* you are. Guilt says, "You made a mistake." Shame says, "You *are* the mistake." I wasn't dealing with something I had done wrong at the luncheon (guilt). I was battling my own thoughts: *I am not a good speaker; I am not adequate* (shame). Healthy guilt has an element of hope attached—an error has been revealed, yet you are hopeful that a positive change will take place as you address your shortcoming. Shame often leaves you feeling helpless—after all, it tells you that something at the very core of your being is defective.

Just as I did not understand the distinction between guilt and shame, I did not realize that there are two kinds of shame. The first, *healthy shame*, prompts you to correct—or prevent—sinful behavior. Good shame reveals that you are not perfect and that you are not God. Healthy shame reminds you that you have limits and that you will make mistakes. It can act like the warning light on your car's dashboard that reads "Maintenance Required." It can help alert you that something is wrong under your hood. So you stop, pay attention to the warning, deal with it, and move on.

For example, when I was six, I started taking accordion lessons. Not long after, my teacher explained that I would be expected to play "Drink to Me Only with Thine Eyes" from memory at my first recital. For some reason (probably because of the title of the song), I procrastinated and hadn't memorized the piece by the time the recital rolled around. Not surprisingly, when I got up to play, I messed up big time. I kept playing the same measure over and over until finally I just stopped playing. There was dead silence. I was very embarrassed. I knew I was supposed to have had that piece memorized, but I had not done it. Thankfully, neither my parents nor my piano teacher berated me after the recital. In fact, my teacher even gave me a little prize at the end of the evening! Still, the good shame I felt pushed me to be sure I worked hard before my next recital.

While my illustration of good shame was from a silly example of childhood, I am concerned about a lack of *good shame* in our culture. The number of babies born outside of marriage, marital affairs, and cheating—whether on tax forms or in the classroom—are all increasing. Unfortunately our culture has a growing tolerance toward these practices. Thousands of years ago the prophet Jeremiah gave a sad commentary on his culture: "They have no shame at all; they do not even know how to blush" (Jeremiah 6:15). We are losing our ability to blush as well. Healthy shame ought to lead us toward repentance and restoration, healing and forgiveness. Good shame, then, does have its place.

What I'm talking about in this book, however, is another type of shame. It's an unhealthy, destructive form that author John Bradshaw calls toxic: "Toxic shame gives you a sense of worthlessness, a sense of failing and falling short as a human being."[1]

The results of toxic shame are serious and long lasting. "People affected by it judge themselves, rather than judging their actions. If they make a mistake or do something wrong, they judge themselves as bad, rather than judging their actions as imperfect. They live in terror of unexpected exposure—of others seeing them as they see themselves."[2]

These were the vague feelings of inner torment I experienced not only every time I got through speaking but in other situations as well. Unfortunately, toxic shame lingers and eventually becomes a part of who you are and what you do and don't do. It paralyzes you so you don't think you can move on.

When I returned home from the luncheon that day, I ran upstairs to the solitude of my bedroom and fell on my face before the Lord. "Please, God, show me if there is shame in my life." Instantly a painful memory surfaced—one I had never shared with anyone except, in part, with my husband. An unpleasant memory from when I was five; a memory I had buried but couldn't forget. It was a secret I had carefully hidden behind a heavy door in my heart for many years. I was still pushing against that door with all my weight to keep it closed.

God came that afternoon, so to speak, and slowly pulled me away from that closet door and gently took me into His arms. I was so tired of trying to keep it closed. I didn't want that door opened, but I couldn't bear putting my weight against it any longer.

He was reassuring and tender as He held me and spoke very clearly to my heart.

Marilyn, it is hard for you to receive compliments. You do not feel like you are ever good enough. You act as though you are "affirmation-deficient"; no amount of affirmation fills you up. You are afraid you'll be abandoned. You feel overly responsible for other people.

At that precise moment, I knew—my outlook on life *was* shame-based. Toxic shame was the reason for my continual vague feelings of uneasiness and inadequacy. The Lord began to reveal to me the secret stash of shame I had carried for many years. He invited me to remove the tinted glasses of shame that blurred and darkened my vision of whom He had called me to be. Gently, the Lord helped me crack open the door of a carefully covered secret memory I did not want to deal with. . . .

Can you relate? Do you ever have a vague, bogged-down feeling that something is wrong with you? Do you ever feel that while you've been told God loves you, He certainly must love others *more* than you? Do you sense that you can't measure up to what people or God want from you? Do fears torment you and keep you from being a confident person?

Perhaps you feel a rush of anger whenever you feel put down so you lash out at the person closest to you. Or you might down an entire half gallon of ice cream after listening to your boss go on and on about how you should improve your time-management skills. Maybe you berate yourself for minor mishaps. Say you accidentally back into a neighbor's mailbox. Even after paying to have it replaced, you *continue* to feel bad about it and indulge in self-berating thoughts. *Why wasn't I paying more attention when I backed out of the driveway? How could I have been so dumb?* And every time you drive by that now-repaired mailbox you wonder how you could have been so brainless to make such an obvious mistake. By way of contrast, people who do *not* view life through the lens of toxic shame may back into a neighbor's mailbox and while they feel bad, they can fix the mailbox and then move on. They do not *continue* to degrade themselves.

Toxic shame can take an outward event (like hearing a critical comment or backing into a mailbox) and turn it *inward*. It causes you to focus on yourself in a negative way. Instead of recognizing that you accidentally hit a mailbox, toxic shame can make you believe that you are a *mailbox hitter* and always will be. If you make a mistake while presenting a workshop for your company or church, you tell yourself, *I'm not a good presenter. I'll never be able to speak again.* You believe the internal message and refuse to give another presentation—even though you are very capable.

Shame is bound up in *who* we are and not so much with *what* we do. Author Stephen Seamands writes, "Shame, though it may be triggered by something we have said or done, is about our *being*."[3]

Many avenues lead to this destructive kind of shame. If you struggle with it, you may have had parents who were shut down emotionally and could not affirm you as a child. You may have been physically, emotionally, or sexually abused. Perhaps you experienced an extremely humiliating and embarrassing situation and were teased about it. Or someone made fun of your body and to this day you can still hear their hurtful comments. These types of experiences breed shame. When this type of shame is stuffed deep inside rather than addressed, it becomes internalized.

Once this toxic shame is internalized, it runs on autopilot. It can be triggered without anyone doing anything to you. Your own thoughts set it off! This toxic shame expresses itself as inner torment. Continual negative self-talk can be a dead giveaway that toxic shame is present in your soul.

Just as shame has many sources, it also manifests itself in different ways. Some people will try to dull the pain through addictions or eating disorders. Others will fly into uncontrollable rage over the smallest slight. Some will sink into depression and withdraw from others. Then there will be those who are so afraid of making a mistake that they fall into the pit of perfectionism. Sadly, "some studies have determined that shame can be a key factor in suicide attempts."[4]

If you struggle with feelings of inadequacy, perhaps, like me, you were not aware of or able to identify the root of these problems as shame. Until now! Dear reader, I long for you to recognize unhealthy, toxic shame in your life. Why? Shame seeks to paralyze you. Shame shuts down your insides. Shame cuts you off from truly giving to and receiving from others. But there is good news. Once you are aware of shame, you can reverse the atrophy. There is a cure! Perhaps you don't struggle with shame but know someone who seems in bondage to an addiction or seeks to live as a perfectionist or is at an emotional standstill in life. Now, maybe, their struggle has a name—toxic *shame*.

The story that follows shows how shame can take root early in life and then, if left alone, grows effortlessly and stubbornly as a weed. Like a weed, it grows inconspicuously at first until later, when it stands taller than the life around it. In my own life, this harvest of shame produced bitterness and negative self-talk. Its most beguiling fruit, however, was that of lies—internal lies. Shame set me up to believe lies about myself—lies from the enemy of my soul. It can do the same to you.

If you or someone you love is struggling with shame, I hope my story serves as a helpful illustration. Obviously, your circumstances will be different than mine. Your shame may have very different roots, and it may not produce the perfectionism or inadequacy that mine did. Yet I suspect that the fear, anger, and disappointment we often feel inside is similar.

This is also a story of what I've learned about pulling out the root of shame and allowing forgiveness, truth, grace, and hope to grow in its place. In fact, I've included "How about You?" questions and action steps, called "Shame Lifters," at the end of each chapter to enable you to identify the ways shame shows up in your life and then take steps to resolve it. Even if you decide not to do the questions and Shame Lifters, I encourage you to at least read through them since other illustrations of shame and hope are scattered through them.

If you're not battling shame personally, these exercises may enable you to be a shame lifter and foster healing in a friend's or family member's life. In addition, turn to the appendixes on pages 189–197, which will help you recognize whether shame is a problem for you or someone you know.

While writing my story was often painful, my hope is that you will see some aspect of your story in mine and then draw even closer to the God who longs to be your ultimate Shame Lifter.

ONE
Fears and Tears

*Human beings are born with just two basic fears. One is
the fear of loud noises. The other is the fear of falling. All
other fears must be learned.*

— Ronald Rood, American naturalist

Fear took hold early in my life. It clung to me like maple syrup
sticks to your hands after you eat pancakes. I tried over and over
again to wash away the fear with my tears, but it didn't work.

"You're always crying. Quit being a crybaby," my father
would often say impatiently. "What is the matter with you, anyway?"

I was dubbed "Crybaby" early on and lived up to my title. I
found the more I cried, however, the more my father distanced
himself from me both physically and emotionally. Crying never
really achieved what I had hoped for, but I couldn't stop myself.

One night when I was four years old, I awoke in my bed and
was immediately consumed with a fear of the darkness. I went
to my parents' room, stood by their bed, and cried. Nothing they
said calmed my fears. "Marilyn, go back to bed," my dad said
more than once. Finally, he threw back the covers on his side of
the bed and started toward me. I felt a firm grip on my upper
arm. My dad pulled me down the hallway to our bathroom and
snapped on the light. He shoved me toward the sink. The cream

tile counter with its dark brown, spotted markings came sharply into focus. The ribbed, frosted windows on either side of the sink glowed from an outdoor light that cast distorted, prism-like patterns on the counter.

"If you are going to keep crying, I'll give you something to really cry about," my dad said. As he pushed my head over the sink, he grabbed a bar of soap and shoved it in my mouth. Over and over he washed my mouth out with the soap. The biting taste repelled me, and I cried harder than ever. I do not remember what happened next, but I do remember this: I was very frightened of my father. Just as the frosted bathroom windows contorted the outside light that was reflected onto the bathroom counter, so my father's actions that night distorted my view of him even more.

I knew deep down my father probably loved me. After all, didn't all daddies love their children? But I didn't feel close to him. In spite of my fear of him, however, something in me longed to please him, and I desperately wanted his approval.

My dad faced huge pressures during my early years. He was a pastor and was gone from home a lot. At the time he washed my mouth out with soap, he was planting a new independent church without receiving an income. He was also working in the early morning hours at our local post office to provide for my mom, older brother, and me as best he could on his meager income.

About this time my parents decided that taking a vacation to visit relatives in Michigan would provide a break from all the stress of church planting. I was five and my brother was thirteen the summer we took that trip from our home in Southern California to Battle Creek, Michigan. By the time we neared the desert town of Barstow, California, I was crying. There were no seat belt laws in that day, so I stood up in the car and leaned over the front seat.

"I want to ride up front," I announced through my tears.

"No, Marilyn," my dad said. "You need to sit back down in your seat."

"But I want to sit up by Mommy," I explained.

"No," was his firm response.

I melted into more tears. My crying continued until the car abruptly stopped on the right shoulder of the road. At that point my crying abruptly stopped as well. *What was happening?* I wondered. The next thing I knew, my dad had gotten out of the car, walked around to my side, and opened the door.

"Get out!" he ordered.

I hesitantly got out and stepped onto a very deserted desert road. My dad reached in the car and pulled out my little suitcase and set it on the road next to me. He then walked back to his car door, got in, slammed the door, and drove off. I watched in utter disbelief as I saw our car getting smaller and smaller on the road until I could no longer see it. I wailed uncontrollably. I was so frightened! I truly felt like he would never come back and get me. I don't know how long I was left there, but I was certain there was no hope of seeing my family again. Sometime later my dad returned for me.

Thankfully, I don't remember any other cars passing by, and I was probably not left there for long. Still, the memory lingers. My dad may have come back for me physically, but emotionally he had left me alongside that desert road.

A new level of fear began to grow in me, and I would wake up crying in the night for my mother even more often. While I could not express it at that time, what I was feeling was fear of abandonment. *What will happen to me if I get left again?*

My fears continued to increase after our trip and into the fall when I started kindergarten. I was so fearful of getting left again that my mother needed to reassure me over and over again that my dad would remember to pick me up from kindergarten. (My mother didn't have a driver's license.) It was at that point I developed my biggest fear of all—that my mother would die and leave me. She was my stabilizer in life, and I clung to her as much as possible.

Shame, mixed with fear, was beginning to send down new and stubborn roots into the soil of my very being. I felt shamed for being called crybaby and a fraidy cat by family members and others. Shame had the incredible power of taking those two phrases and weaving them into the fabric of my life. I believed and internalized those phrases until they became *me.* Instead of "shame on you," I picked up the mantle of shame and it became "shame on me."

Something *was* making me cry. I was carrying a deep, dark secret. It left me fearful, overly sensitive, and worried. Also, the fear of being left alone followed me just like my shadow did.

What *was* the matter? I couldn't talk about it. So I cried instead. It seemed the more I cried, however, the less it helped; but still I couldn't quit. Tears were somewhat like a comfortable addiction—crying felt good and temporarily relieved some of my anxiety, but it never quenched my soul pain.

My kindergarten teacher observed my tears as well. She informed my mother that I was fearful, lacked confidence, and cried easily. I overheard her tell my mom this as I sat nearby playing on the rug in her classroom during a parent-teacher conference. Later I asked my mom what the teacher meant by her words about me.

"Well, honey, your teacher said you are capable of doing the schoolwork, but many times *you* don't think you can. You need to have the confidence to go ahead and try."

Could I tell my mom at that point about my fears? Could I tell her that because she couldn't pick me up from school,

I was extremely afraid my dad would forget to pick me up after kindergarten? No, that sounded silly.

Could I tell her that my teacher frightened me when she yelled at the class and how I thought she wasn't very kind? Could I tell her about a girl in my class named Donna, who accidentally wet her pants during school? The teacher made an example out of her. First she announced to the class what Donna had done. Then she made a pair of panties out of paper towels and tape and held it up for the class to view. Donna was red faced, and I was humiliated for her. I didn't ask why Donna wasn't at school the next day or any other day after that. I felt her embarrassment. I knew why she never returned to school.

Could I also tell my mother about that *secret thing* that had happened to me months earlier, which had frightened me more than anything else? No! I decided not to share the fear that was troubling and paralyzing me. I didn't want anyone to find out my secret. It would be safer that way. And so I cried and rocked myself to sleep each night. Those were the only ways I knew how to cope with my growing fears. My tears were simply voicing the unspoken fearful words of my fettered and cheerless heart.

HOW ABOUT YOU?

1. Can you identify with having an emotionally distant parent? If so, how has that impacted your life?

2. Do you remember ever being shamed as a child? If so, how would you complete the following sentence:
   I felt shamed when I _____.

3. Psalm 39:12 (NLT) says, "Hear my prayer, O LORD! Listen to my cries for help! Don't ignore my tears." (By the way, *ongoing* tears may be an indicator that something more is going on inside.) How do you typically express your hurt? How might you bring your shame or disappointment to God?

4. Have you ever felt hindered by hurtful, destructive words or names that were said over you as a small child? What were some of them?

5. Do you now have freedom from those words, or do they still have their paralyzing grip on you today? Explain.

6. Are you dealing with any past or current fears? In what way?

7. In Isaiah 41:13 (NLT) God promises, "I hold you by your right hand—I, the LORD your God. And I say to you, 'Don't be afraid. I am here to help you." What hope does this passage offer you?

✳ ✳ SHAME *Lifters* ✳ ✳

- Identify a secret that you have been holding on to or an ache that just doesn't go away.
- Why do you want to keep this secret hidden? Why do you think the ache persists?
- Identify a person you could safely confide in. Pray for the courage and wisdom to bring this secret or hidden ache out into the light.

Dear heavenly Father,

Thank You for listening to my cries when I call out in the "darkness" of my soul to You. You cry with me and take note of my tears (Psalm 55:17; 56:8).

Thank You that You do not leave me by the side of the road in my daily struggles. You are there for me. You are emotionally and spiritually connected to me! Even if I don't recognize Your presence, You do not leave me—nor are You ever in the process of leaving me (Hebrews 13:5). You will not, nor cannot, leave me as an orphan (John 14:18). Over and over You speak peace to my heart and say, "Do not fear; I will help you" (Isaiah 41:13).

Thank You that Your name for me is "beloved." Your words never wound to destroy me. You speak only healing words of conviction, comfort, and encouragement. You value me and treat me with dignity.

Heavenly Father, You love me with an everlasting love (Jeremiah 31:3)—the kind of love I know so little about, but desire to experience more. Thank You! In the name of Jesus, Amen.

TWO

*L*oved like *C*razy

Infinitely loved . . . as I am! Not as I will be, or could be or might have been, but just the way I am this minute.

—Elizabeth Sherrill

My secret fear was safe with me. I put it in a closet of my heart, shut the door, and locked it. For extra measure I put my whole weight against the door, intending to keep it closed—forever. Shame encourages you to hide painful experiences.

I did not realize at the time how my secret would impact and control the next forty-seven years of my life. It encouraged me to withhold part of myself. I believed I could not fully disclose myself to others even if they were safe. How I wished I could have brought myself to tell my secret to my mom, the one person I trusted most, but I just couldn't.

Fear whispered to me that if I told her my secret, I would not only greatly disappoint her, but I would also lose her love. I believed that lie. Even though I knew my mother was a safe person, there was such fear surrounding my secret it literally paralyzed me from telling her. How could anyone—even my mother—love a bad little girl like me?

Looking back, I know I was viewing myself through hazy, tinted lenses of shame. Unfortunately, those lenses distorted my view of my mom. Sadly, shame affects not only what *you think* about yourself, but also what *you think others think* of you. She had no idea of what I had gone through or the fearful thoughts that tormented me. While I'm sure my mother noticed some of my fears since I obviously lacked confidence, we never talked about the *source* of those fears. It was the 1950s, and such conversations were not as common as they are today. Yet I know if I had gone to her with my fears, she would have immediately helped me.

But why didn't my mom stand up to my dad the day he left me on the side of the road? Again, I think much of it has to do with the era. Back then, such assertiveness by a wife would have been out of place. Yet I'm beginning to see that perhaps there was something deeper going on under the surface as well. I remember when I was younger asking my mother why she married my father. All she would say was, "He was a good man," with a hint of a smile. Whether her reticence toward my father was socially conditioned or whether she was struggling with something in her own past, I will never know, since she passed away years ago. I do know, however, that in every other type of situation my mother was there for me, and her love was deep and affirming.

To try to build my self-confidence, my mom enrolled me in all kinds of musical instrument classes, baton and ballet lessons, and even a military-type camp. Unfortunately, my feelings of shame were so strong that it was difficult to have any confidence in myself. As a young girl I never really could move forward and speak up. I was like a hot air balloon that's all fired up and ready to lift off but can't go anywhere because it is still tightly tethered to the ground. The ropes needed to be cut.

Shameful thinking always darkens and distorts truth. So at the age of five, I made some decisions to protect myself. First, I would try hard to forget what had happened to me. (It's that old "buck up without dealing with it" philosophy.) Second, because

I loved my mother and I knew she loved me, I would try very hard to be a good girl. I thought these actions would erase the bad feelings I had about my secret. Finally, I would stay as close to my mother as possible, which was very easy to do. And because she was so nurturing and loving, I was eventually able to push down my shame until my early teen years. By refusing to think about my secret and depending more and more on my mother, I was able to get some short-term relief from the secret that plagued me. Since then I've learned that research confirms that a child who lives with even one loving nurturer in his or her life has the ability to become a *resilient* child.[1]

What made my mom the kind of parent a child wanted to be close to? She was easy to be with, personable, and patient. She had a great sense of humor and laughed easily. My brother and I still have fond memories of hearing our mother laugh. There were times when she would be in the middle of disciplining my older brother and they would somehow both end up laughing.

My brother adored her. While my father never so much as tossed a football with him, my mother played ongoing Monopoly and Scrabble games and made sure she was available.

Her parenting style was especially winsome to me because it contrasted so sharply with my father's nonengaging style. If my father asked me to get him a tool from his workbench in the garage and I couldn't find it, he would get angry. He'd stomp to his workbench, pick up the tool I had failed to see, wave it, and exclaim, "If it were a snake, it would bite you." I remember thinking, *I hope if I have children someday and I ask them to find something for me that I will be patient like my mother.*

She connected with all three of her children on a deep emotional level. (I have a sister twenty years older than me who was married shortly after I was born. My mother was forty-five when she gave birth to me, so I was a bit of a surprise, to say the least. Never once, though, did she make me feel like I was a mistake or not wanted.) Each of us adored her and was greatly influenced by her.

While she did not give me all the material things I wanted, my mother gave me what children want most from a parent— she gave me herself. She gave me her time.

Don't get me wrong; she was not perfect and she knew it. She admitted her mistakes and asked for forgiveness when needed. I loved that about her. I know personally how hard it is to admit, "I'm wrong," or "I am sorry." She was also quick to forgive me after I had genuinely asked for her forgiveness. She did not remind me of my offense or hold it against me.

She had a contagious love for God that not only affected the way she talked to God, but also the way she interacted with people. I wanted to love Jesus simply because she did. She followed hard after Him, and I wanted to grow up to be just like her.

I also remember thinking at a young age how I wanted to be a parent like her because I loved how she parented me. She chose to see the humor in situations. She was creative and very intentional about making the most of any teaching opportunity.

"Mommy, why do the birds sing so loudly in the morning? They always wake me up."

"Oh, honey," she said with a smile, "they all gather together right before the sun comes up to sing praises to the Lord! We could all learn a lesson from them! Next time they wake you up early in the morning with their singing, see if you can think of something you can praise the Lord for."

Whether it was praising the Lord with the birds or seeing God's creativity in the clouds, my mother taught me to remember to look for God in my day ("God sightings," as I later heard a friend describe them). She explained that God shows up every day; however, we don't always recognize Him.

Once when I was around eleven, a teen from our church asked my mom to go to a shop with her to pick out a prom dress. I got to go along. The teen tried on a couple of different dresses when all of a sudden I noticed she was crying. My mother spoke to her in gentle and hushed tones. Finally, my mother turned to me and said, "Honey, would you mind waiting for me on a chair near the dressing rooms? I'll explain later." I sat and sat. Eventually, the teary-eyed teen and my mother, with her arm around her, emerged from the dressing room area.

When we got home my mother sat down with me and shared what happened during our shopping trip. "Honey, while I was in the dressing room with Linda, I learned she was pregnant." My eyes got big. I knew Linda was only sixteen and not married.

My mother did what I thought was an amazing thing. Without ever saying anything negative about Linda or putting her down, she used that experience as an opportunity to talk to me about waiting to have sex until I got married. I believe what spoke to me most was my mother's compassion for Linda. There was no condemnation. My mother was not a shame giver, but rather a *shame lifter*. Although Linda felt deep shame and humiliation, my mother helped restore her dignity. She continued to love and support Linda throughout her pregnancy. A shame lifter gives grace to the disgraced.

Not many months later, my mother brought another unwed teen into our home, allowing her to stay for a few months during her pregnancy. "I believe Jesus wants us to help and care for her," my mom told me. Once again, she viewed this as a teaching opportunity for me.

My mom's gentle reminders to be compassionate impacted me as well. One time as we waited in our car at a red light, an obese man walked in the crosswalk in front of us. Someone in the backseat of the car snickered and made a negative comment.

I remember my mother saying, "Let's make it our goal, myself included, never to make a hurtful comment about someone we see on the street. We have no idea what they have been through and we must respect them. If we say negative things about them—even though they cannot hear us—it shows we think we are better than they are."

She set similar standards at home. "We are not going to use the words *stupid, dumb,* or *shut up* in this family," my mother announced one day.

Another way she taught me to respect myself and others was by reminding me that God made me the way I was for a reason. When I was in fourth grade, I wrote her a note about wishing I was someone else. I listed several names of people I would rather be and left it on her pillow. They were all people of great accomplishment and talent. She wrote a note in return and left it on my pillow. Beside each of the names I had listed she wrote: "I am glad you are not this person!"

She went on to write how happy she was that I was just who God made me to be. Later on this lesson was reinforced for me as a teen when I read Galatians 6:4: "Let everyone be sure that he is doing his very best, for then he will have the personal satis-faction of work well done, and *won't need to compare himself with someone else*" (TLB, italics mine). As soon as I read that I wrote a note to myself in the margin of my Bible right next to that verse: "Be you!"

Mother taught me about self-acceptance on other occasions as well. "Marilyn, what are you doing?" my puzzled mother asked me one afternoon.

"I put a clothespin on my nose to see if I could change it," I explained. "I don't like my nose."

My mother had a faint smile on her face. It must have been comical for her to see me walking around our house with a clothespin on my nose. Actually, I was in great pain from that clothespin and I didn't know how much longer I could stand to keep it clamped on my nose.

"Honey, that really makes me sad that you don't like your nose."

"What?" I exclaimed as I took off the clothespin. "Why should *you* feel sad? You don't have *my* nose."

"Oh, but in a way I do," my mother countered. "You see, you are part of me so that means some of your nose is from me. It's like you are telling me you don't like *my* nose."

Quickly I replied, "But, Mother, I like *your* nose."

"And I like *yours*—just the way it is. Marilyn, you were created by Jesus and He gave you your nose. If you say you don't like your nose, do you think it may make Jesus sad?"

I hadn't thought about it like that before. I knew when I made a little ceramic pot at my elementary school I would have been hurt if someone told me they thought my creation was ugly. I put the clothespin back in the clothespin bag. Several times after that incident, my mother told me, "Honey, whatever people think in their hearts is what they become." I'd remember those words, adapted from Proverbs 23:7 (NKJV) later in life.

At about this time a man in my parents' church was very upset with my mom about something that had happened at church. I never knew exactly why he was so angry or what my mother had done to offend him. My mother tried several times to talk with him. She asked him what she could do to help, but he was too angry to talk and eventually left the church. It was never resolved in her lifetime.

Years later, I found a letter in her desk written to that man. It was not sealed, so I opened the envelope and pulled out her heartfelt letter of apology. She was asking the man to forgive her and not to turn his back on God because of her.

Our family decided to mail the letter to this man even though years before he had not wanted to accept my mother's forgiveness. Her letter ended up profoundly affecting him. It brought him back to church, but even better it brought him back to God.

Probably the most important thing my mom gave me was her unconditional love. She did not let a day slip by without saying, "I love you." Those were words I longed to hear from my dad, but for some reason he was unable to voice those feelings. My mother knew the power of those three words. She knew they enabled one's soul to thrive even as food is to the body. She also knew the power of touch and consequently hugs were given daily. My mom had parents who loved and treasured her, so she was raised with affection. She was simply passing down what had been given to her.

My mom told me a story (which happened many years before I was born) that would ultimately affect the rest of her parenting years.

A mother and teenaged daughter who were part of my parents' congregation had been fighting one morning. They normally walked down the street together to go to school and work. This particular morning as they walked they continued to argue. Finally they came to an intersection where the mom was to turn one way for her job and the daughter needed to turn the other way for school. As the mom stepped off the curb she looked at her daughter and continued the argument. Suddenly this mom was hit by an oncoming car and was killed instantly. Later that day the teen ended up at my parents' home. She cried uncontrollably as my mom held her.

"I didn't have a chance to tell her I loved her," she said as she continued to sob. "We were fighting and now she's gone."

My mother said she vowed right then not to let a day go by without telling family members around her that she loved them. She stuck to her promise.

That love also played out in the way she carefully disciplined me. My mother's discipline was *consistent*, which I have since discovered can be so tiring. (Sometimes it's just easier to let the issue slide!) Plus, her discipline was done in a *caring* fashion. I not only knew my boundaries with her, I also knew her expectations of me. On the other hand, my dad, instead of disciplining me, punished me. His method was to spank me with a belt—which thankfully was rare since I tried so hard to be good.

My mother was an on-site parent and an intentional teacher. She had not only physical and emotional goals for her children, she also had spiritual goals. She knew that each child was born an eternal being and was created for eternity. In that light, she saw her children as a mission field. She prayed and longed for Christ to be "fully developed" in our lives (Galatians 4:19, NLT). She knew she could not, by her power or authority, *make* her children love God. So she sought to lead us to God by living as close to Jesus as she possibly could. She was a student of her children. She made it her job and privilege to pray daily for us. (Her written prayer journals, which I now have, are a testimony to this fact. I love opening her journals and seeing my name written on a page and the way she was praying for me. What an incredible spiritual inheritance she left us.)

Even though we did not have much money, she managed every so often to bring home what she called "prizes"—little surprise gifts like a small white wallet, a piece of candy, or piano sheet music. I never knew when she would bring home a prize, but when she did, it was a big deal for me. Her prizes said, "I was thinking about you."

She made me feel treasured by spending time with me. And I learned later that a person who is treasured does not feel the effects of shame as intensely as one who is not cared for. I truly felt cherished by her.

My mother would often leave encouraging notes on my pillow or slip a note written on a napkin into my lunch bag. She modeled God's love for me. The lesson she wanted me to learn from her love was that we are also treasured and valued by our heavenly Father: "I am my beloved's and I am the one he desires" (Song of Solomon 7:10, TLB). I loved her like crazy, and I knew, without any doubt, I was loved like crazy by her.

HOW ABOUT YOU?

1. What were your mom and/or dad's parenting styles like? How did they encourage you? Did they ever do anything to discourage you? If so, what?

2. What is the most nurturing thing someone (a parent, teacher, coach, etc.) did for you as a child?

3. Have you ever had an opportunity to come alongside someone who feels humiliated and shamed? What did you do to help that person?

4. Proverbs 10:7 says, "The memory of the righteous will be a blessing, but the name of the wicked will rot." What can you do to ensure that after you die your memories will bring a blessing to the next generation?

5. How do you tell your family members "I love you"?

The following questions are specifically for you if you are a parent:

6. How has your parents' parenting style personally affected *your* parenting style?

7. Based on your actions, do your children hear you say, "I'm crazy about you" *or* "You're driving me crazy"? Explain.

8. One of the best ways to ensure your kids aren't burdened by shame is to begin teaching them early about God's great love for them. My mother did this through her consistent love and nurturing. She also spent one-on-one times with me going through fun Bible workbooks. How could you help your kids begin to feel confident about God's love for them?

9. The psalmist talks about the importance of making our homes safe places: "I will try to walk a blameless path, but how I need your help, *especially in my own home, where I long to act as I should*" (Psalm 101:2, TLB, italics mine). In what ways can you ensure your home is a "safe" home and a nurturing place?

10. What comes to your mind when you realize the child entrusted to your care—whether he or she is your biological, adopted, or foster-care child—is truly *God's* child?

❋ ❋ SHAME *Lifters* ❋ ❋

- Is there a single parent or a child from a single-parent home whom you could help? You could spend time with such a child once a month or reach out to help a single parent. A small group from our church invited a group of young single moms who have a hard time making ends meet to a local Laundromat. The group told these women to bring all their dirty clothes. Our people put quarters into the machines and helped the moms wash and fold all their clothes. They also brought in homemade cookies and treats for the moms and their children as they waited for their clothes to dry. The moms expressed their gratitude over and over. They felt so loved and cared for.

- If you are a parent and your child is old enough, surprise him or her with a small prize when you come home. Tell your child, "This is just because you were in my thoughts today and I love you."

- If your child (or grandchild) is two or older, schedule an inexpensive one-on-one "date time" with him or her once a month. (Make it very simple and inexpensive—a trip to a playground, ice cream place, or a donut shop.) When they enter their teen years, it is a natural way to continue connecting with them. My husband did this with each of our five children. We called them "Christy Days," "Holly Days," etc. Our kids have happy memories of these times.

- Pray for your child. Probably no one else will pray for them more than you.

Dear heavenly Father,
We are reminded that while there are no perfect earthly parents or per-
fect children, there is one perfect parent—You. Not even the best parent
on earth even begins to compare with You (Matthew 7:11).

How wonderful that You long to partner with me in my everyday
living as well as in my parenting. I am not alone. Even when I mess
up, I can acknowledge my mistakes and You stand ready to help
(1 John 1:9).

Continue to remind me that although I may not have been loved
the way I would have liked, Your love for me is complete, full, and
abundant. There is no love like Yours (Psalm 36:7-10).

Remind me that the way I love the children under my influence
directly impacts the way they understand Your love for them (Deuter-
onomy 6:5-7).

Thank You for leaving Your parenting manual—the Bible—on
earth for us. It is living, active, God-breathed, and current for today's
challenges (2 Timothy 3:16-17). Help me to be the kind of parent,
grandparent, aunt, uncle, or friend that makes it easy for children to
come to know Jesus at an early age. I pray that these children, with
Your help, will impact the next generation (Psalm 78:3-4).

May I daily follow closely behind You, remembering that I have a
whole line of children, teens, and adults watching and following me
(1 Corinthians 11:1). In Jesus' name, Amen.

THREE

Good-Bye, My Love

Everything that has truly enhanced and enlightened my
existence has been through affliction and not through
happiness.

—Malcolm Muggeridge, *A Twentieth Century Testimony*

Treasured, valued, and loved like crazy! I wanted so much to feel that from my father too. For some reason, however, I didn't, and I couldn't figure out why. I eventually gave up trying to figure out my dad and stayed as close to my mother as possible. When I needed something, I asked my mother rather than my dad. I learned to stay out of his way. My dad was gone a lot, which only reinforced my dependency on my mom.

When I was nine my mother was hospitalized at the UCLA Medical Center. I was told she needed to have an operation, and I would have to stay with a family from our church. No one told me what kind of surgery she was going to have. I asked but was given only vague answers. Only later did I learn she was battling breast cancer.

It seemed as if she was in the hospital a long time. Finally she came home, and I was told she needed to rest. She moved into our family room and stayed on the pull-out sofa. As a result, we had much time together. I could count on finding her there when I came home from school. We talked about many things.

And I wasn't the only one who stopped by to talk to her. Many times when I came home from school, one or more women would be at her bedside talking to her. One day I came home to find a woman sitting next to my mother with a handgun nearby. I was about to say something when I got the look from my mom that said, *Don't say anything. I'll tell you later.* I learned the woman had come to tell my mother that she had lost all hope and was going to shoot herself. My mother talked to this despondent person, helping her know that Jesus loved her. As a result of my mother's counsel, that woman came to believe in Jesus Christ that day. Many others sought her bedside wisdom, too, including a well-known movie star at that time, Dale Evans Rogers, wife of the cowboy actor Roy Rogers. There was something about my mom. I wasn't the only one who enjoyed and benefited by being around her.

Gradually her strength returned. She resumed teaching two women's Bible studies, carried on her duties as chaplain of my school's PTO, and served in a counselor/advisor position for a group of prominent Christian women. I noticed, however, that she needed to rest each day, which concerned me, but I never talked to her about it. I remember wondering if all moms needed to take a nap in the middle of the day.

Five years later, when I was fourteen, my mother told me she needed to go back to UCLA for more tests. It was routine for her to go to the doctor every few months, so I wasn't overly concerned.

She was packing her suitcase for the hospital on a Wednesday night as I was getting ready for a youth group service at our church. "Marilyn, you mean you are going to go to youth group and leave me alone the night before I go to the hospital?"

I looked at her but saw a twinkle in her eye and knew she really wasn't serious. She knew I liked a boy who was going to be at youth group that night. Before I could respond, she said, laughing, "You go right ahead. I'm glad you enjoy going to church."

As my mother was getting ready to leave for the hospital the next day she said cheerily, "Honey, I'll just be gone for the weekend."

Normally, she would go to the hospital for a few hours. This time, however, she was scheduled to stay for three days. When she noticed the skeptical expression on my face, she hugged me.

"I'm only going in for some routine tests," she reassured me.

That night I found a note on my pillow (which I have to this day):

> My dearest Marilyn . . . Sleep tight tonight. Hug the pillow and pretend it's me—I'll do the same. Put yourself in God's care and let Him give you rest and peace for all will be well. Love and prayers always for my baby! Mother.

"All will be well," the note said. But it wasn't well at all. The weekend slipped into Monday, then into Tuesday. Day after day my mother remained in the hospital.

"Dad, when is Mother coming home?"

"Oh, soon—she just needs some of Grandma's chicken soup and she'll be fine," my dad would say. As the days turned into weeks, I kept asking my dad when she was coming home. The answer was always the same, "She just needs Grandma's soup to get her strength back."

"Dad, may I please see her at the hospital?"

"Marilyn, the hospital won't let you in. You have to be sixteen and you are only fourteen."

"Please, Dad, could you ask if I could have special permission to see Mom?" I begged.

Finally, my dad asked the nurses if I could visit. Thankfully, I was given permission to see her anytime I wanted. For my first visit, my dad told me to wear heels and put my hair up so I would look older. I had not seen my mother for over two weeks and was very excited about being with her. My joy faded, however, the moment I saw her. She smiled at me from her hospital bed, but she looked so different. She was very thin, and her skin was stretched tightly on her body. Her cheeks were hollow, and her bones seemed to stick out on her legs. Gingerly I went over to her bed.

"Hi, Mother. I miss you so much."

"Hello, honey," came my mother's loving but weak voice.

I chose not to mention how terrible she looked. I wanted so desperately to believe that, in time, she would be okay. No one explained what was wrong with her, and for some reason since family members weren't talking about it, I decided not to push for answers.

I do remember asking the doctors for updates when they came into her room. The standard answer was, "She's holding her own." I assumed that was good news. With that in mind, I truly believed God was going to heal her and give her back to me.

I spent a couple of weeks going back and forth from the hospital. It was tiring, but I kept going, hoping and praying I would see improvement. My mom and I spent our time talking with each other about school and life. She also asked me to read Scripture to her from *Living Letters*, a new biblical paraphrase of Paul's epistles. Often as I read to her, she would, by memory, say the verses with me. She had whole chapters memorized. I savored these times.

Finally, after my mother had been in the hospital for over a month and a half, I was told she was coming home. It was incredibly good news. I had prayed so earnestly for this as I knelt by my bed and prayed for her every night. I just *knew* God was going to heal her! I had mustered up more faith than I ever had before and even told my sister that God was going to do a miracle and heal Mother. With fresh assurance of her healing, I reminded the Lord, as I bargained with Him, that I needed her at home and He needed her on earth too. Surely He wanted her to get back to teaching her two Bible study classes.

The day my mother came home from the hospital, we had everything ready for her. My dad had even gone out and purchased a new refrigerator! She had wanted one for a long time because our old one kept breaking down. That was enough reassurance for me to believe she was going to be okay. Why else would he buy a refrigerator?

We put her on one of our patio chaise lounge chairs with wheels and rolled her around our house. She wanted to see every room. Family and friends came to see her, and it was a very happy day for me.

"Marilyn, honey, I would love to hear some of the piano pieces you have been working on while I was in the hospital."

One request she had made in her note before she left for the hospital was that I remember to practice every day after school. She said it would help fill some of the lonely hours while she was gone.

I got out my piano book and played one piece for her as she rested on the lounge chair near the piano.

"That was wonderful, honey. Please keep playing."

So I did. I played every piece I knew, mistakes and all, with her murmuring affirmations about each one.

I truly did not know the storm that was brewing on that day. I thought God was returning her to us to stay home. Later that day, my mother was wheeled into our family room, where she was placed on the sofa pull-out bed. One by one family members took turns going in to talk with her. They always closed the door behind them.

My sister told me that Mother wanted to talk to me, so I went into the room and sat on the bed by her. Someone closed the door. I looked intently into her eyes. I saw what I would describe as a sweet sadness in her dark, chocolate-brown, tired eyes. She smiled at me, and as if searching for the right words, reached out her frail hand to me. I sat as close to her as I could on the bed and held her hand.

"Honey, my disease isn't going to heal," my mother gently said.

I let her words sink in for only a moment before I threw my body on top of hers and blurted out, "No, no! I don't want you to go. No, it's not true. Why doesn't God heal you?" All my pent-up denial came gushing out through loud crying. She held me as tightly as she could while I sobbed.

"Why, Mother? Why doesn't God heal you?" I questioned repeatedly.

"Honey, I really don't know," she answered softly. She then added carefully, "I do know that the Lord has assured me that you will be okay."

Her statement that I was going to be okay made me dizzy. While she hadn't said those words harshly, my thoughts were thrown into chaos. I remember thinking God was wrong. How could He assure my mother I would be okay? Besides, I thought He had assured *me* that He was going to let her live. I was so confused.

She continued to talk with me about her love for me and gave me some last instructions. She also talked about my future husband and my future children.

"Marilyn, I had asked the Lord to let me live until you got

married and had children. However, since I now won't be able to meet your husband or hold your babies in my arms, I have been 'holding' them in prayer. I have been praying for your future husband and your future children."

It is amazing to me that she had the foresight to tell me she had been praying for the next generation. You pay attention to a person's last words, and her words about prayer and praying for the next generation continue to impact me. Even as she was dying, she was living out Psalm 145:4: "One generation will commend your works to another; they will tell of your mighty acts."

I spent the rest of my one-on-one time with my mother cuddled up next to her on the bed, my arms wrapped around her—I did not want to let her go.

My mother made sure she spent individual time with each of her three children on that day she came home from the hospital. As the afternoon wore on, however, even I could tell my mother was not doing well. She struggled to breathe in spite of her oxygen tank. She needed to get back to the hospital quickly.

My family loaded her into our pale yellow and white Pontiac station wagon and made the half-hour trip back to the UCLA medical unit. After we arrived, the nurses got her comfortable, and I stood by her hospital bed holding her hand. She looked so peaceful now.

"Come on, Marilyn, it's time to go," my dad said wearily.

Reluctantly, yet as bravely as I could, I bent down and kissed my mother good-bye. Her eyes glistened as she said good night to me. I turned and walked out of her room. As I walked down the dimly lit green hospital corridor, I had a compelling desire to run back to her room.

"Just a minute, Dad, I need to kiss Mother one more time."

I quickly ran back to her room. My mother, surprised but pleased, smiled at me.

"I'm not going to school tomorrow, so I will come see you in the morning, okay?"

My mother smiled faintly again and whispered, "Okay, honey, I'll see you tomorrow morning."

I kissed her again and returned home with my dad. I was so glad I had kissed her again. That was the last time I saw her alive.

The phone sounded unusually loud and jarring the next morning when it rang around 6:30. I tiptoed down the hallway to see who could be calling so early. I heard my dad say, "She did? When?"

I knew then that my mother was gone. Gone for good. Great sadness engulfed me like I had never known before. I ran to my dad and threw my arms around him.

"Daddy, Daddy, I don't know what I'll do without her," I sobbed as I embraced him.

My father did something that jolted me. He pushed me away from him, looked me in the eye, and said, "Marilyn, you just have to go on. You just have to go on."

Confusion blurred my thoughts for a moment. Why was my dad pushing me away from him, especially at a time like this? Why did he tell me I had to go on? All I wanted was for my dad to hold me and cry with me. I desperately wanted his comfort, but instead I received a strong message that I just needed to buck up. I was shamed for having needs, so I assumed there must be something wrong with me. Dazed by his rejection, I ran to my bedroom and cried.

"Marilyn," my dad called as he knocked at my bedroom door, "there is no use staying at home and crying all day; there isn't anything you can do. I think you should go to school today."

I know I was in a bit of shock, but I do not know what

possessed me to go to school, other than I knew my dad wanted me to go. He dropped me off at school, and I sat silently in my first two classes. I was afraid if I said anything I would start crying.

I made it to my third-hour drama class. The teacher called on me to get up on the stage and perform a scene from a play we had been working on, but I couldn't do it. The teacher, thinking I wasn't prepared, asked, "Why aren't you ready?"

I looked at him and burst into tears. "My mother just died," I said in front of the entire class.

For a moment my teacher's eyes looked angry. "What in the world are you doing here at school?" he demanded. Without waiting for an answer, he continued, "I want you to go to the office, call someone to pick you up, and go home."

Almost in a zombielike state I went to the office and called home. A relative came and drove me home.

I immediately ran outside into our backyard and looked up at the blue, cloudless September sky.

"God," I cried out, "I don't know what to do. I don't know how I can make it without my mother."

"God, if You are really real, I need . . . I need," I repeated hesitantly, "I need You to be a *mother* to me."

There, it was out! I wasn't sure if it was okay even to pray that way, but I didn't care. I didn't need a *Father* God. I needed a *Mother* God. A God who would love me like my mother did. I needed a God who would nurture and love me. I did not want an aloof God like my dad. I was absolutely desperate and did not know how else to tell God what I needed.

For fourteen years my mother had told me about God, taught me songs about God, and prayed with me. I liked the God my mother followed and worshiped. I was fascinated with the way He seemed to answer many of her prayers and the way He was so real to her. But I didn't feel *good enough* to have that kind of relationship with God. And because I didn't feel good enough, I thought I would not be pleasing to God. Consequently I believed God did not want to be close to me just as my dad didn't want to be close to me. An aloof earthly father meant an aloof heavenly Father.

But now I was desperate for God. My father had pushed me away. Maybe my heavenly Father would also push me away, but I needed to know for sure.

"God, I need You, please help me," I pleaded in my backyard. "I need You to fill up an empty space inside of me. I'm scared and I feel so alone."

In that intense lonely moment, something incredible happened. I felt embraced by my heavenly Father for the very first time. It was very real. He did not push me away like my dad had done. As He held me, an incredible peace began to wash over me like a gentle rain. I couldn't explain what was happening, but I actually had a quiet awareness of His presence. It seemed as if I could actually feel Him standing there with me.

That experience was to determine the path I eventually chose. I was at a crossroad that day: I could either take a path of bitterness and continue on in anger at God for taking my mother or take a step toward God and believe that He would actually help a frightened fourteen-year-old.

At that moment, I chose to trust the God my mother loved. Because God had extended His grace to me, I accepted Him as fully as I could and started to lean hard on Him. I began to transfer my dependence from my mother to my heavenly Father on that September afternoon.

The day of my mother's funeral arrived, and over five hundred people packed out our church. A huge spray of red roses with a ribbon banner that read "Beloved Counselor" covered the top of her casket. Her many friends had purchased those roses.

My brother, who had been fighting in the Vietnam War just a few days before, was able to attend the funeral. The Red Cross had found him on the battlefield and told him that his mom was dying. They flew him home a couple of days before her death, but he had to return to Vietnam right after the service.

After the funeral everyone began to leave. My brother had to go back to the war; my married sister needed to get back to her family. The church people went back to their lives. I remember feeling that the world needed to stop. My mother had just died, so why did everyone just go on with life as if nothing had happened? Then my dad decided to take a trip to northern California. He took a leave of absence for a month and left me behind. Again, I felt abandoned. It was strange how even though my dad and I were not close, I still wanted him to stay home with me. Once again I felt left like I was left along the side of a road.

"God, where are You?" I cried. "Are You going to be a mother to me?"

Thankfully, the Lord answered that prayer by sending an aunt to me who had arrived from Michigan right before my mother died. Although my aunt Ellen had planned to leave immediately after the funeral, when she saw my situation she decided to stay and care for me that first month while my dad was gone.

Aunt Ellen was very loving, and I was starved for an affectionate touch. She listened to me and made home-cooked meals. We even went clothes shopping together—just like my mother and I had done. My aunt and I remained close after her extended stay, even though we lived thousands of miles apart. She sent me little gifts and notes of encouragement. I truly felt as if God had sent an angel-mom into my life.

After my aunt Ellen returned home, I was left with just my dad. There was an awkward uncomfortableness between us. My dad didn't know what to do with me. I overheard him saying to my sister who was visiting one day, "All Marilyn wants to do is hang on me."

"Dad, all Marilyn wants is to be comforted by you," my sister explained. "It's okay that she wants that from you."

Our house was quiet. I missed my mother praying with me every morning before I left for school. I missed her notes in my school lunch. I missed walking in from school each day and hearing her call out, "Hi, honey." I missed her laughter. I missed the little "prizes" she'd bring home for me from the store or when she had been away at a speaking event. I missed the notes she would leave for me on my pillow. I missed the times she would sometimes crawl in bed with me just to talk for a few minutes.

I was to learn that grieving is a process—a long process. I also learned that the closer you are emotionally to a person, the greater the grieving. Grieving has two parts. First, you grieve hard when the person you dearly love dies. Then you grieve as you have to learn to live life without that loved one. In other words, there is the initial grief of losing a loved one and then the long-term grief of living without him or her. I had to learn to live life without my mother.

Two months after my mother died, I was still secretly crying about her death. I thought I would be called a baby if people knew I continued to cry over my mom. I used to wonder if the crying would ever stop. *Why are people happy?* I wondered when I'd see groups of people laughing and having a good time. *Don't they know I've lost my mother?*

During this time I happened to be at my girlfriend's house as she and her mother were arguing over some silly thing. Their fighting escalated until I couldn't stand there any longer as a silent witness.

"Please stop fighting," I demanded over the volume of their angry voices.

Suddenly there was silence as the mother and daughter turned to look at me.

"Please don't fight," I said again, this time in a whisper. "At least you have each other. I would give anything to be able to talk to my mother. Don't waste your time fighting with each other."

My friend and her mother nodded their heads, agreeing to end the fight as they saw me standing there shaking and obviously distraught.

It is so hard to lose a loved one. You never know what is going to set off your emotions. Grief crashes like a wave on the shore of your soul and then rides back out on the tide—only to come crashing back into your thoughts again.

I remember sitting in church one day and writing in very tiny letters in the back of my Bible, "I miss Mother!" I was embarrassed and didn't want anyone to know that I was still grieving, but I had to get it out somehow. My note was dated November 13—just about two months after my mother had died. Recently I pulled out that Bible from my shelf and looked at those words written in pencil by a very sad fourteen-year-old. I now realize that my grief was silently contributing to the reemergence of my feelings of shame. *What would people think of me if they knew I still cry and feel sad?* I would ask myself. *I'd better hide my true feelings and make people believe everything is fine.*

For a few months after my mother's death, her clothes remained in her closet. Almost every day I would open her closet door, grab as many of her clothes in my arms as possible, and hug them. I would drink in deeply the lingering yet fading fragrance of her inexpensive perfume, *Evening in Paris*. It made me feel I was almost normal when I did that—like I still had a mother. I was fighting feelings of shame, thinking that now I was only half a person and that people were probably feeling sorry for me because I was, in my estimate, an orphan. People didn't know what to say to me. It's strange, but I *wanted* to talk about my mother's death. I got the feeling, however, that people wanted to avoid the subject and talk about other things. There were no grief counselors in that day. Not one teacher or administrator from my school ever talked to me about my mother's death. I would have loved it if someone there had said, "Tell me more about your mother," or "Could I share a special memory I have of your mother with you?" or even, "Do you feel like talking about your mother today?"

Thankfully, not everyone avoided me. A woman by the name of Ruth Harms Calkin reached out to me in a special way. She wrote me a note once a month for a year after my mother died. I finally confessed to her that I couldn't quit crying. I remember her tender response back to me, "Marilyn, let the tears fall. One day God will take those tears and shine His light through them and make rainbows." In other words, Ruth gave me permission to cry without feeling shame.

Somehow life has to go on after the death of a loved one. So I found myself thinking a lot about heaven. It became more real to me because a part of me was already there. I also had frequent dreams of my mother. She looked healthy and radiant and was no longer ravaged by cancer. I believe this comfort came from my heavenly Father.

My mother showed me that preparing for death is one of the most important jobs we have while we are living. We are all born eternal beings. We are not temporary. My mother had lived much in her short fifty-nine years. Some of her final words to my sister were, "Honey, I have shown you how to live like a Christian, and now I want to show you how to die as a Christian."

I also saw, as she was dying, that there was nothing I could do. No amount of money could heal her; no fame or success could restore her, not even if I had more faith . . . nothing! I felt so helpless.

I could only release my mother and then run into the arms of a God whose love, I hoped, was stronger than death.

HOW ABOUT YOU?

1. Have you experienced the loss of a loved one to whom you were emotionally close? If so, describe some of the feelings you experienced then—or are experiencing now.

2. Is there someone you could come close to as they go through a difficult grieving time, like Aunt Ellen and Ruth Harms Calkin did for me? What encouragement might you offer?

3. "But to all who believed [God] and accepted him, he gave the right to become children of God," according to John 1:12 (NLT). No matter what difficulties we go through, God loves us as His children and longs to have a relationship with us. What next step will you take to begin—or grow in—your relationship with Christ?

4. Can you recall a time of being shamed for having needs or shamed for your feelings? Describe.

5. The apostle Paul encouraged the church in Corinth to "follow my example, as I follow the example of Christ" (1 Corinthians 11:1). Those words are loaded with responsibility! Do others listen and desire to follow you because they see you following hard after Jesus, or do your life and words discourage and hinder them? Explain.

✳ ✳ SHAME Lifters ✳ ✳

- If you know a child or teen who has recently lost a parent, send them a card once a month for a year. (If you need to, put it down on your calendar to remind yourself.) Remember the date their parent died and make sure you connect with them a year later. Believe me, if that child is old enough, he or she is remembering and thinking about that day. You can do the same for a person who has lost his or her spouse or child. Send a card a year later. My husband does this with people in our church and so often he hears, "How nice to know that you remembered this date."

- Make a commitment to mentor a child or teen who has lost a loved one. Not sure you can mentor? If you can be a friend, you can do it. My mother used to mentor me every Saturday morning with a Bible sticker book. I missed that focused attention after she died. It would have been so meaningful to me to have had a woman come alongside me to pick up that activity.

- If *you* have lost a loved one, have the courage to confide in a trusted friend when you approach special dates (birthdays, anniversaries, etc.). Allow that person to minister to you when these difficult and lonely days approach.

Dear heavenly Father,

Your Word says that You collect all my tears in Your bottle (Psalm 56:8, NLT). I matter to You and I truly am Your beloved child. Thank You that one day You will wipe away all my tears, sorrows, and pain (Revelation 21:4). Until that time, I fix my eyes on You, the One who has already conquered my last enemy—death (Hebrews 12:2). You are the living God who understands what it is like to grieve and feel abandoned. Your Word says that You are a "man of sorrows, acquainted with deepest grief" (Isaiah 53:3, NLT).

Thank You that You come alongside the hurting (Psalm 109:31). Thank You that You are preparing a place in heaven for those who have made a decision to accept You as their Lord and Savior (John 14:2-3).

Please help me as I seek to follow You while I am on earth. Help me keep just enough of the lowlands of heaven in view to give me a needed perspective of eternity (Ecclesiastes 3:11). In the name of our risen Savior, Jesus Christ, Amen.

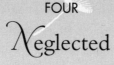

FOUR

Neglected

Neglect, indifference, forgetfulness, ignorance are all impossible to [God]. He knows everything. He cares about everything. He can manage everything. And He loves us!

—Hannah Whitall Smith

Right before the casket lid was closed on my mother's body, I kissed her one last time. I was told later that was a morbid thing to do, but it helped me move toward closure. I said good-bye to the person I loved the most on earth and at the same time resolved to tuck my dark secret into the coffin with her. A little later, I stood back while my dad opened the door of the hearse as the pallbearers loaded her casket. I remember someone saying later, "That was the first time I've seen him open a door for her."

My dad and I were stuck with each other like unwanted gum on the bottom of a shoe. He was without a wife, and I was without a mother. Silently we wondered what to do. Neither of us, however, asked the questions that needed to be asked. Who would take me to my junior high school three miles away? How would my dad juggle pastoring a church and caring for a daughter at the same time? Who would make dinner?

"Marilyn," my dad asked when he came home from the church office one evening, "didn't you start supper?"

"Dad, I didn't know what to make," I explained.

"Well, what have you been doing since you got home from school?" he asked.

"Uh, I practiced my piano lesson, did some homework, and nothing much else."

"You've been watching TV, haven't you?" Without waiting for an answer from me, he stormed over to our TV and placed his hand on it. "The television feels hot. You've been watching TV for a long time," he fumed. "Marilyn, you should take some responsibility around here. Quit watching TV and start something for dinner when you come home from school."

"Dad, I don't know how to cook or where to begin, but if you'll give me instructions and buy the food, I'll try to get the dinner started."

"Oh, never mind," he muttered.

Instead, we began going to a small diner near our home almost every night for dinner that first year after my mom died. While I lived on their hamburgers, my dad developed an ulcer, which he blamed on "that greasy spoon."

I tried to please my dad as much as possible. That meant making sure I turned off the TV long before he got home. I didn't want him to think I was lazy.

I was also careful about asking him for piano lesson money. I would wait until the last second to ask him. "Dad, I need money for my piano lesson today."

With a disgusted look, my dad would get out his wallet, pull out a bill, and say to me, "This is my last five dollars." Each week, my dad made it a big deal that I was taking his money. I concluded from his behavior and words that I was a burden to him. I cringed any time I had to ask my dad for money.

It had been so different with my mother. "Honey, get the money for your piano lesson from the jar in the cupboard," she'd say. Whenever my mother taught a ladies Bible study, the women gave her a love offering. She used that money to pay for my lessons, but that jar was empty now.

At age twelve, I had begun playing the piano at church whenever we didn't have a regular pianist to play during congregational singing and for the choir. I wasn't throwing my dad's piano money down the drain, but he made me feel like I was. While my mother would encourage me if I played in a Sunday service, my dad would say, "Marilyn, quit playing the piano so softly and put some oomph into it."

Getting a ride to and from school also became a definite problem. I went to a junior high in another school district. Before my mom died, a neighbor had driven me to school. When she no longer had kids at that school, I no longer had a ride. My dad was not used to taking me or picking me up from school, and he kept forgetting to pick me up. Day after day I waited outside school for him. Finally, I would go back into the office and ask if I could use the phone to call my dad.

"Dad, where are you?" I'd complain.

"Oh, I totally forgot. I was involved with something here at church."

This pattern continued for months. Deep down it triggered my old abandonment fears. I was afraid of being left by my dad again. I've heard that babies are born with only two fears—loud noises and being dropped. By age fourteen I had added many new fears, and they were growing stronger every day.

Then my fifteenth birthday arrived. As I waited for my dad to pick me up after school that day, I thought how glad I was that I only had five months left at my junior high, which would end my worry about my dad forgetting me. In the fall I would be able to walk to and from my new high school. But it was my first birthday without my mom and I was a bit melancholy. I felt so alone, and for the first time I was dreading my birthday. My mother had made birthdays special for each of her children. It was a day when she made it clear she was glad we were born. Author Rick Richardson says, "Birthday celebrations are not tied to anything we have done or accomplished; birthdays celebrate that we *are*."[1]

After a lengthy wait outside, I went into the school office and called my dad. I couldn't reach him. Finally the school secretary told me to wait inside while she made some calls. She eventually reached my dad and handed me the phone.

"Oh, Marilyn, I will be right there! I was doing a funeral and just finished the graveside service. I'll be there as soon as I can." I had totally slipped his mind.

As I got in the car, my dad asked if it would be okay to go over to the home of the deceased. The family was hosting a dinner for all those who were at the funeral.

"Dad, it's my birthday!"

"I know," answered my dad, "but I really think we should be supportive to the grieving family members."

Compliantly I went along and celebrated my first birthday after the death of my mom by attending a funeral supper.

My fears and feelings of abandonment only continued. In subsequent months our relationship continued to be rocky. My dad was clearly uncomfortable parenting a fifteen-year-old girl. He used some odd and graceless phrases that stuck with me. If I said I was going to a friend's house he would remind me not to stay too long. "Don't wear out your welcome. Remember, 'Withdraw thy foot from thy neighbour's house; lest he be weary of thee'" he'd say, quoting Proverbs 25:17 from the King James Version. I often wondered whether I was overstaying my welcome when I was a guest at someone's house. I also worried that I was a burden to my dad.

"Marilyn, don't be a follower. Be a leader!" was another admonition I heard often from my dad. How much better it would have been if he had said, "I see leadership potential in you." That would have spurred me on! Instead I heard in my head, *Marilyn, you will never be a leader; you'll only be a follower.* I began to view myself as an inferior person who did not have the ability to be the kind of pastor's daughter my dad wanted.

Then my dad, in an effort to "help" me become a leader, told me I needed to get a job to earn money and gain confidence.

"Since you are on spring break I want you to go downtown and find a job *today*," he said emphatically one Saturday.

I protested, "But, Dad, how do I get downtown to apply for a job? Don't I have to be sixteen to work at a store?" I was doing babysitting in the neighborhood, but the pay was pretty low.

"You're not too young, and you can walk the mile to our downtown" was his solution.

My niece, who was four years younger than me, happened to be visiting during that spring break. She offered to walk downtown with me. We went in one store after another. Each of the store managers asked the same two questions: "How old are you?" and "Do you have any experience?" I returned home later in the afternoon without a job and no place else to apply. My dad was very angry.

"Marilyn, I'm grounding you. You need to stay in your room for the rest of the afternoon and night."

"But, Dad," I said, "I really did try to get a job. No one wanted to hire me."

My niece also chimed in her support. "Grandpa, please don't ground Marilyn. It's not fair; she tried! Besides, you promised you would take us miniature golfing tonight."

I reminded my dad again that I had inquired at lots of stores and had filled out applications. "Dad, I've never been grounded before," I added, hoping he would change his punishment.

"You're grounded, and that's final. And we're not going miniature golfing, either," he said adamantly.

I went into my bedroom and shut the door. My niece sat outside the closed door, crying, "It isn't fair, it isn't fair." I, too, felt the unfairness, yet at the same time I wondered what was wrong with me that I couldn't secure a job to make my father proud of me.

My dad was bringing back to the surface all the feelings of shame I thought I'd buried. The messages he unintentionally communicated to me were: "You don't measure up. You're not a leader. You're lazy. You're not responsible. Don't be a burden to anyone. You cry too much. You're not confident."

I allowed his negative messages to play in my head. I couldn't erase them no matter how hard I tried. I wish I had known that, while I might not be able to erase them, there was a way to *eject* them. (I'll explain what I mean in chapter 11.)

I truly do not think he was intentionally being a shame giver, but because of things in his past he passed his shame on to me. That's what happens when you don't recognize shame and get rid of it. You pass it down. While my dad unknowingly became a *shame giver*, I, at the same time, unknowingly became a *shame receiver*. (See the appendixes on pages 189 and 193 for a complete description of shame givers and shame receivers.) When shame givers send you negative messages, they really think they're helping you and doing you a favor. They have a twisted sense of responsibility. They think it is their responsibility to fix you, but they do it in a negative way, assuming that will get your attention better than if they did it in a positive way.

I love what my daughter Holly does with her three-year-old daughter, Ella, if she starts to whine. Holly gets down on her level and looks into her eyes. Very calmly she says, "Ella, I need you to stop for a minute and use your words to tell me what you want." Holly has done this enough times now that Ella knows that if she stops whining and uses her words, her mom will listen and respond to her. Holly is in the process of "fixing" Ella, but she is doing it in a careful and loving manner. Holly is giving Ella the message that she and her feelings matter.

I recently heard author and speaker Gail MacDonald talk about the impact of negative "childhood names" that were given to us. Mine was "crybaby." It proved to be an unconstructive way to try to fix me. If a nickname or negative words from your childhood haunt you, they may still have a shaming power over you. Sadly, it's possible that you took those messages and believed them until they became *you*.

So what are some clues to recognizing a shame giver? You can identify shame givers *by the way they listen to you* and *the words they use*. First, look at the way a shame giver listens to you. They are not good listeners. They may hear your words, but they do not hear your heart. They are listening to you only so they may try to "fix" the problem instead of *listening to understand* where you are coming from. There is a big difference between "listening to fix" and "listening to understand."

Had my dad truly listened to me when I came home without a job, he would have "heard" that I really did try. He might have sat down and brainstormed some job possibilities with me. My dad, however, thought that by grounding me, I'd learn a lesson in being responsible. He wanted to fix me. He was much more interested in my performance than in who I was.

Shame givers also interrupt. They will not allow you to finish a sentence. While you are talking, they are planning what they will say back to you. They can't wait to give you *their* thoughts, opinions, and commentary. Many times when I tried to reason with my dad, he would simply say I was being "argumentative" and end the discussion.

Shame givers' words also tend to be discouraging. They frequently use the word *should*. When someone tells you, "You should . . . ," you are not being given much choice in the matter. Often when a person uses "should," they are revealing their own personal opinion. They make it sound, however, like everyone wants you to do what they are telling you. "You should have ironed your shirt. What will people in the office think?"

Shame givers also communicate an "I know better than you" attitude. "You should have known better than to speed on that road. I just knew you'd get a ticket one day." Unfortunately, their words (which might even be expressing truth) have a way of tearing down rather than building up. If you have done something wrong and gotten "caught," you probably already feel bad about it. Shame givers rub it in, while at the same time, they think their advice is helping you. They have no idea that their advice is actually damaging and does the exact opposite of what they want.

Shame givers use phrases like, "What would your friends think of you if they knew . . . ?"; "You look sloppy today"; "You're worthless"; "Keep your big mouth shut"; "What's wrong with your brain, anyway?"; "What would your father think if he were around?"; "You're a liar"; "When I was your age I always got A's." They have a way of labeling you.

Shame givers are quick to give out put-downs. Just recently a man told my pastor husband, "That was a great sermon this past Sunday, but the three before that weren't so good. They didn't do anything for me." His words certainly did not edify or build Paul up.

Shame givers can sound like scolding parents. They lecture you to make their point, but often feel the need to go on and on. Even though you are an adult, you feel like a little child as they loom over you with all their words. You want to plug your ears and cry out, "Stop! Too many words, too many words."

Another characteristic of shame givers is the way they make negative comments without considering their words before they say them. Many women have told me that their dad, mom, or some other person in their lives said to them at mealtime, "My, you sure are piling the food on the plate. You're getting a little pudgy, aren't you?" Don't misunderstand; I know parents need to be concerned about their kids' diets, but the way in which we voice those concerns is crucial. Sadly, inappropriate comments like "You're getting a little pudgy, aren't you?" can be labeled as shame talk and can eventually push people into eating disorders.

Shame can be communicated in many disguised ways as well. It can come through a dirty look, a hand signal that says "go away," or the rolling of the eyes. It also happens when you are talking to someone who purposely walks out of the room to disengage from you. He or she is treating you as if you are invisible.

Shame can result when shame givers compare others too. I heard a gal share a very positive comment about her husband with a group of women. "He gives me a gift every day. It's not a wrapped gift. He gives me a gift of prayer." She went on to say, "My husband made a commitment ten years ago to pray with me every morning before he went to work, and he has kept that promise."

That is a wonderful gift! But another woman who heard this story later said to me, "When I get home I'm going to tell my husband, 'Do you know what Jim does for Kate every day before he goes to work? He prays with her, and he's been doing it for ten years! Why don't you do that for me?'" Ouch! When spouses or children feel as if they're being compared to others (and found wanting), feelings of shame often result. I believe a better way for that woman to state her feelings to her husband would have been, "Honey, I would love it if we could pray together each morning. Would that be something you would be interested in?" If he said yes, then great. If no, they could discuss it again later. But it's not productive to use comparisons to manipulate our spouses or children to do something.

Shame givers also think that you need to hear their advice and that it's okay for them to be brutally honest. I value and welcome honesty, but truth needs to be balanced with grace. I remember the extended family get-together where our two-year-old daughter decided to throw a temper tantrum as we were leaving. I was a fairly new parent doing the best I could in dealing with her when a family member came up to me with a smirk and said in front of the others, "My, my, she has a temper, doesn't she? What a strong-willed child you have!" My husband and I both felt embarrassed, and I interpreted the comment to mean I was a bad parent. How much better if he had said with a smile, "I remember those days; I've been there with my own children. It's part of dealing with a two-year-old. Just hang in there." Instead, the words we heard were: "Shame on you parents for not being able to control your daughter."

I've noticed that shame givers also sometimes make negative comments that end with, "I was only kidding. Can't you take a joke?" By then, however, the damage is done. The person to whom the negative comment was directed not only feels bad about what was said but realizes he or she is also perceived as not being flexible enough to take a joke. It's a double slam.

Years ago my husband and I were out with some couples for dinner. During the dinner, one friend, Victor, looked at one of the women in our group and said, "Did you notice that one of

Shar's eyes is smaller than the other?" There was an immediate awkward silence. Shar looked surprised and reached for her purse to grab a small hand mirror. I happened to look at Victor's wife. She had stiffened and was mortified her husband had said something negative about Shar.

As soon as Shar got out her mirror, Victor started laughing and said, "I was only kidding. Come on, you've got to be able to take a little joke." Shar not only felt embarrassed about the comment, she also felt dumb that she didn't realize he had been joking. Sadly, however, there was some truth to Victor's comment. If you looked very closely you could see that one of Shar's eyes was a tiny bit smaller than the other. Victor had made a true statement in jest—another mark of a shame giver.

The invalidations shame givers make can be subtle or overt—even severely abusive. All can be very damaging. Their put-downs or abuse can even be aided by a shame enabler—someone who is aware of the mistreatment but does nothing.

The words of a shame giver remind me of the old toothpaste tube illustration. You can squeeze the paste out of the tube, but it's another thing to try to shove it back. The same is true of our words. Once they're out—they're out! A shame giver's words communicate, "You don't matter at all—only what you *do* and how you do it matters to me."

HOW ABOUT YOU?

1. When my mother died, I resolved to bury my dark secret with her in her casket. Have you ever tried to bury a secret or your feelings, hoping they would never be brought to life again? If so, how well did that work?

2. Were any childhood names or labels (positive or negative) attached to you when you were growing up? If so, how have they affected you? If they were negative, take heart! God says one day He will give each of His children a new name—and every one of those names will be good (Revelation 2:17).

3. Author Rick Richardson writes, "If as you were growing up your birthday was forgotten or minimized, you may well have very little sense of celebration that you are and that your existence is to be rejoiced over." Were you celebrated on your birthdays? If not, what can you do on future birthdays to help you remember your birthday is special to God—after all He planned you before you were born? Psalm 139:16 (TLB) tells us, "You saw me before I was born and scheduled each day of my life before I began to breathe. Every day was recorded in your Book!"

4. Can you identify any shame givers in your life?

5. What are some healthy ways you can reject their shame messages so you do not fall into the trap of being a "shame receiver"?

6. Have you ever caught *yourself* being a shame giver? (I have.) What can you do differently to guard against slipping into that behavior again?

7. My friend Sherry Harney called recently and asked if I could meet her at a coffee shop. I presumed she wanted to share something with me. It turns out she scheduled the time for me to talk and her to listen to me! I kept trying to turn the conversation back to her. "No, this is your time to talk," she replied sweetly. What a meaningful and rare gift she gave to me.

8. How would you rate your ability to listen to someone? Great_____ Good _____ Okay_____ Fair_____ Poor_____ Improving_____.

What might you do to improve your listening skills?

❋ ❋ SHAME *Lifters* ❋ ❋

- Pay close attention this week to the messages you tell yourself. Are they encouraging, the kind you might use with a friend? If not, the Bible is a great place to go to find out how precious you are to God. (See, for example, Psalm 139:13-16; Matthew 10:29-31; and Ephesians 2:10.) Begin repeating one of these passages to yourself instead.

- The next time you need to tell someone what to do (whether it is a child or an employee) *listen to your own words*. Are you communicating that you care about that individual as a person or only about his or her performance?

- Practice listening this week. Here's an easy tip to get started: Recently a reading specialist told me the importance of listening when reading to a young child. She gave this example: "When you point to a picture of a flower on a page and ask, 'What color is this flower?' wait at least four seconds for the child to answer. Don't jump in earlier and give the answer. Wait!" That's good advice whether we're listening to kids or adults. Four seconds sounds so short, but when you are waiting for someone to answer, it seems so long.

- Begin working at becoming a shame lifter. That may mean you refrain from telling someone the idea he or she just shared with you is far-fetched and unrealistic. Instead say, "Tell me more about your idea. How do you see that working out?" A shame lifter allows another person to express himself or herself without giving advice. When asked for advice, seasoned shame lifters usually say, "Tell me why you are asking" instead of immediately jumping in and giving advice.

- Set up a time to meet with a friend or family member. Once you meet, tell him or her that you'd like this to be a time for *them* to talk. Keep the conversation focused on the other person. If you need help getting started, ask a question like, "So, what have you been thinking about the most lately?"

- If someone has verbally shamed you (and you're quick enough to catch it), try saying back to that person: "Would you please rephrase that statement so it doesn't come across so threatening to me?" Sometimes that helps a person understand that his or her words are destructive.

- Write a love note to someone you are close to. Express your appreciation not for what they do, but who they are.
- Keep track of how often you say "I was only kidding" in a given day. Strive to speak with grace (which is another word for love) and truth, leaving no doubt about the sincerity of your words.

Dear heavenly Father,

Thank You that the messages You give to me, Your child, are positive and meant to build me up (Isaiah 61:1-3).

You knew, however, that there would be times when people would tear me down with their words and actions. How good it is that You invite me to come to You and to hear Your words spoken over me (Zephaniah 3:17). They are words of life, never words of shame.

Thank You for always listening to me. Help me to be a better listener to You and to others (James 1:19). Remind me, dear Father, because sometimes I forget to listen (Psalm 46:10).

You know that my heart searches for identity. I need to hear my true identity and name from You (John 10:3). Do not let me assume labels from anyone else! Please remind me that I am valuable apart from my performance. In the name of Jesus, the name above all other names, Amen.

FIVE

Loss after Loss

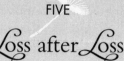

*I'm overwhelmed with sorrow! sunk in a swamp of
despair! . . . But me, I'm not giving up. I'm sticking
around to see what God will do. I'm waiting for God to
make things right. I'm counting on God to listen to me.*

Micah 7:1, 7, *The Message*

My dad and I continued trying to learn the dance of living
together without stepping on each other's toes. He didn't know
how to live with his daughter, and I didn't know how to live
with my dad. We were like two strangers.

Late one night I woke up and heard muffled sounds. I got
up from bed and quietly moved toward the sounds. I went to
a closet and opened the door. My dad was in the closet on the
phone.

"Dad, what are you doing in the closet?" I whispered.

He said a hasty "good-bye" to the person he was talking with,
hung up, and looked at me.

"I was talking with a woman named Elizabeth."

"Dad, is something going on between you two?" I asked, surprised.

"Well, yes, I've just started talking to her in the last month.
I'm lonely, and she's a widow, you know."

I knew Elizabeth. She was a pleasant woman with a round face and curly brown hair. She had been my third grade Sunday school teacher. I was just surprised that my dad was calling her only six months after my mom's death.

"Marilyn, I don't want the congregation to know about this yet. So don't say anything."

A bit dazed, I went back to bed and realized my dad had found someone else. I had such mixed emotions. Betrayal! How could my dad desert my mother? I wasn't sure if my mother would have approved. I was still very protective of her and her place in the family. But I could also tell my dad was lonely. Elizabeth would be a comfort to him. It was incredibly confusing.

Things happened quickly between them, and soon they told me they would be getting married in the fall. They were married shortly before the first-year anniversary of my mother's death. My stepmom had never had children, and I, of course, had never had a stepmom. We could have used some family counseling to help us know how to blend our three personalities together. No one thought of that, however.

The wedding arrived, and our home life was pretty good at first. We were all trying to work together. My stepmom actually remembered to pick me up from school after my late afternoon drill team practice, which was a relief after the many times my dad had forgotten me. She was also a great cook. She insisted, to my delight, that my dad purchase a dishwasher for our kitchen. My sixteenth birthday arrived, and she made a German chocolate cake from scratch and bought me new clothes. It was the first bright spot in a very long time.

Our relationship began deteriorating, however, soon after my birthday. My stepmom retired from her job, which meant an immediate and significant loss in our income. Soon after, I asked if I could get my driver's license.

"No, Marilyn, Elizabeth and I don't think you are responsible enough to drive, and we don't have the money for car insurance."

"But, Dad, all my friends are getting their licenses. I completed and passed driver's training, and I'm all set to get my license."

"I said no," my dad firmly repeated.

I begged and begged, but my dad would not give in. I finally gave up.

Months went by, and I saw how happy my dad and stepmom seemed to be. I, however, was miserable. It seemed to me that my dad and stepmom were a team and I was left out. I tried to hold on to the memories of my own mother as much as possible.

One evening my stepmom and I were hand washing some special dinnerware. Holding up one of the dishes, I remarked, "These dishes used to belong to my mother. I remember when the ladies in the church gave them to her as a gift."

Elizabeth turned to me, her blue eyes flashing with hurt and anger. She announced, "Well, these are *my* dishes now." She emphasized the word *my* very clearly.

My first thoughts after she said that were, *I will never bring up these dishes again; I feel like I have lost another connection to my mom.* I came home from school one day soon after that to discover that all my mother's things had been sold and moved out. With a few exceptions (some items had accidentally been left in cupboards), most everything was gone.

"Dad, I didn't know you were going to sell Mother's things. I didn't get to keep some things I wanted," I lamented.

"Well, I needed to get your mother's things out of the house, so I had a buyer come in and take everything."

I ran in and out of rooms looking to see what was missing.

I opened my brother's closet and couldn't believe what I saw—or I should say, didn't see.

"Dad, where are Cliff's clothes?" I yelled.

My brother had left his clothes in his closet, intending to use them when he returned from Vietnam.

"Dad, where are Cliff's clothes?" I repeated in a panicked voice. For me, seeing his clothes in the closet had been a comfort. It made me think he would survive the war, come home, and wear his clothes again.

In a tired voice my dad explained that he had sold them with the rest of my mother's things.

"How could you do that?" I demanded. "He is going to need his clothes when he gets home!"

In fact, when my brother did return from Vietnam, one of the first questions he asked me was, "Marilyn, where are my clothes?"

"Cliff, I'm sorry, but Dad got rid of them when I was at school." His look was incredulous.

"How could he do that?"

"I don't know" was all I could muster.

As it turned out, the Lord had done something special. In the closet in our family room, which was the room my mother stayed in right before she died, my brother found one of his jackets. Evidently, before my mom died, she had removed the jacket from my brother's closet and put it in the closet where she was convalescing. My brother, seeing his only remaining piece of clothing, quickly pulled it out. A few days later he wore the jacket and happened to slip his hands into the pockets. He felt a piece of paper and pulled it out. It was a note from my mother, saying that she had been praying for his safety in the war and talking to God about his relationship with the Lord. That note greatly encouraged my brother on his spiritual walk. In fact, it was the note that turned him back to God.

Other than seeing glimpses of God like this every so often, however, life was strained. Nothing made sense to me.

For instance, my stepmom made it clear that she did not like dogs, especially in the house. Now that was a problem because we had a five-pound, nine-year-old Chihuahua. I was told the dog had to go. I felt as if Buttons was the only thing I had left of my mother's. Buttons had loved my mom, and I was Buttons' second choice. I'll never forget the day I watched Buttons being taken out of our home. I learned later that she died shortly after that. I was heartbroken. My thoughts were all jumbled up. *Why do I allow people to run over me with their decisions? How come this happens over and over? Maybe my needs are not important after all.*

I understand now my stepmom's need to make my dad's house her home, but I didn't understand what was happening then. My feelings and needs didn't seem to matter, so I stopped trying to express them.

My stepmom, in spite of our issues, wasn't a mean-spirited person. In fact, she was known as a very pleasant woman. But before marrying my dad she had been single for a long time and was used to doing what she wanted. We were both battling for turf, and in a sense, we were also battling for my dad. My father found himself smack-dab in the middle of a battle, and he rightly sided with his new wife.

Meanwhile the tension at our church, the one my dad had started thirteen years earlier, was mounting. I don't know what caused the trouble, but it culminated in a visit to our home by a very angry trustee. My dad was out in the garage when he arrived. I could hear the trustee yelling from inside our house. I stepped outside just in time to hear the trustee swear at my dad. Whatever had happened between them, my dad resigned from the church right then.

Since our church had been an independent ministry,

unaffiliated with any denomination, my dad's job prospects were uncertain. He was left for many months with no income and no place to go. It always amazed me, though, how either a check arrived in the mail or someone brought us groceries at just the right time—more glimpses of God in a dark time. I found out later that our total income for that year was two thousand dollars.

In September we sold our home and moved to a small apartment. We had lived there a month when my dad was hired by another church three hours away. I was a senior in high school, scheduled to graduate in January.

"Dad, do we have to move right now?" I asked. "I only have three months of school left before I graduate." Because of my parents' financial situation, however, they said they needed to move immediately.

"Marilyn," my dad said shortly after receiving the call to the other church, "if you want to stay here, *you'll* have to find a family who will take you in."

I wondered who would take me now that our church family had dissolved. Finally a friend from school told me I could move into her parents' home while she was at college. I did not know her parents, but they graciously agreed to take me in. My parents dropped me off at my friend's house and told her parents that they would send a check each month to go toward groceries.

As I unpacked my belongings, my host family's younger daughter was listening to the radio in her bedroom down the hall. I remember hearing the lyrics, "I'm leaving on a jet plane . . . don't know when I'll be back again. . . ."[1] Old feelings of abandonment crept up again. I felt "left," not sure if my parents would return. Why did I want my dad to take care of me? Why did I want him to tell me he loved me? Why did I continually want from him what he never seemed to be able to give? Why did I keep hoping and expecting him to change?

My dad sent only one month's check for food. The following month the host family asked me why my parents had not sent them the money they promised. I didn't know what to say. They said they were surprised, and I felt embarrassed. I apologized profusely and tried not to eat too much of their food. They didn't ask about a check for groceries the third month because they realized they wouldn't be receiving it.

I did not see my dad and stepmom until two months after they dropped me off at this family's home. My sister invited all of us to her house for Christmas. At that time I talked to my parents about the possibility of going to college. I had done all the necessary college prep work and knew which college I wanted to attend.

"We're sorry, Marilyn, but we do not have money to send you to college." Subject closed.

Thankfully, my sister knew my situation and offered to drive me to the college to talk to their admissions counselor and see if there were any financial aid options.

"Maybe you are eligible for a scholarship," she said encouragingly. Joyce took me to tour the campus, and I knew right away I wanted to attend. I was offered a music scholarship, and arrangements were made for me to do a work-study program and take out a college loan. When the financial aid office found out that my parents were not contributing any money, I learned I was also eligible for a grant from the state of California. My dreams were coming true—I was accepted at Azusa Pacific College (now University). I would start in January right after I graduated from high school, just in time for the beginning of Azusa's second semester.

"Dad, I got accepted at Azusa Pacific," I announced excitedly in a phone call to him. "Also, I'm graduating from high school in a few weeks and I was wondering if you and Elizabeth are coming to my graduation."

"No, it will not work out for us to be there," my dad quickly told me. "This new church needs me right now."

Feeling dejected, I hung up the phone. Work always seemed to come first for my dad. I was dating someone at that time, and when his mother found out my parents were not planning on attending my graduation she acted very surprised. Immediately she asked me if I would go out to dinner with her family following the graduation ceremony.

My graduation night arrived, and I was astonished to receive the highest service award from the principal. As I sat holding the small trophy, my thoughts turned inward: *I wish my dad were here tonight; maybe* this *award would make him proud of me. This award proves I can be a leader.* How desperately I wanted his approval. As I was leaving the ceremony, I spotted my parents in the crowd! I couldn't believe it. I ran to my dad and stepmom.

"Dad, you told me you and Elizabeth weren't able to come to my graduation."

"Well, we changed our minds at the last minute," he said rather nonchalantly. "We came with some of Elizabeth's relatives, and we've made reservations at a restaurant for dinner."

"Dad," I said in exasperation, "you made it very clear you could not come to my graduation and now I have other dinner plans!"

As my dad walked away from me he said, "Fine, you go ahead with your dinner plans, but I'm going out to eat with Elizabeth's relatives."

My dad and I seemed to have what I would call a *dislocated* relationship. It wasn't totally broken or severed, but it was way out of joint and needed to be put back into place—a healthy father-daughter position. Why did I always feel so sad when I was around him? Though I went out to dinner at a beautiful, expensive restaurant with my boyfriend's family, all I really wanted was my dad.

That was it—no graduation dinner with my parents, no card, and no gift. High school was over, and I found myself feeling even more alone. I was also hesitant to ask people to help me. I felt I was a burden to my dad and didn't want to be a burden to others as well.

That same weekend I realized I had no one to help me move to college. I still was not allowed to get my driver's license. I had graduated from high school on a Friday night and was supposed to start college on Monday morning. I had asked my dad if he could help me move to college because my host family lived two hours away from the college. Again, my dad said he was too busy.

Finally I called my sister and asked if she could come and help me move to my dorm room. Even though that would mean a four-hour round-trip for her she said, "Of course I'll help you."

The song "Bridge over Troubled Waters" was playing on my new roommate's stereo as I unpacked. Once again hot tears flowed down my cheeks as I tried to drown out my extreme feelings of aloneness; my waters were truly troubled. Later that evening I walked outside my hillside dorm room and looked down into the San Gabriel valley. Lights glittered like jewels as far as my eyes could see. It was spectacular. Above was the sky with its myriad of stars, which seemed to mirror the image of the valley's lights below.

"God, I need You. Please help me. You say in the Bible that You call each star by name" I cried out, referring to Psalm 147:4. "Do You see me? Do You know my name?"

A few days after settling into my dorm, I realized I had some time before the shuttle bus would take me from the hillside campus to the cafeteria on the main campus. I knelt by my bed and begged God to help me and to work in my life. I had an unusual experience with God during that time. I felt His presence. It was like a warm blanket wrapped so tightly around me that I couldn't move. I felt His love and His acceptance of me as His child. There was a keen sense that He was real and present in that very room. I felt absolutely no shame, no condemnation, only a sweet peace.

I lost all sense of time, and by the time I finished praying it was way past the dinner hour. Nothing like that had ever happened to me before. The shuttle bus had come, honked, and gone. I never heard it. What I did hear was a sweet impression from the Lord. He affirmed me for who I was. It was one of those times when God was like a mother to me, just like I had asked Him to be.

I enjoyed college life, and eventually the campus felt like home to me. Other than occasional phone conversations with my dad, I pretty much went on with life without him. As I approached my nineteenth birthday, however, I was surprised to realize how much I wanted my dad to remember my birthday. My birthday came and went. No phone call and no birthday card. A few days later, though, my dad called. I was pleased! My first thought was, *He remembered my birthday!*

"Marilyn," my dad began, "I know you recently turned nineteen. Now that you are on your own I want you to know that you cannot come back to live at home. Elizabeth and I do not have room for you."

I couldn't say anything for a moment. Had I just heard my dad say I couldn't go home?

"Dad," I replied with disbelief, "you know I am supposed to come home this summer. I have a job all lined up. My boss is expecting me, plus you know I need to work to earn money for the fall semester!"

"Well, you can't live at home, and that's just the way it is."

I heard little else that he said that evening. His earlier words had lodged in my heart, and I hung up the phone in a daze. It felt as if the floor had dropped out from underneath me, just like on one of those spinning amusement park rides where you stick to the wall as the floor drops below you. Thoughts quickly swirled in my head . . . *How would I afford living in the dorm during the summer? Where could I get another job?* I had no idea where to go. But the thought, *My dad doesn't want me,* hit the hardest. Nauseating waves of rejection crashed over me. I wanted off the ride!

Surely my dad had made a mistake. I wasn't into drugs or alcohol, and I didn't smoke. I wasn't running with a wild crowd, I rationalized. Why couldn't I go home for the summer? If anything, I continually tried to be the "good girl," always trying to please daddy.

I called my sister and through many tears told her about our father's decision. Joyce cried with me. She knew it didn't do any good to try and talk to him because his mind was made up. After she talked to me for a while and I calmed down, she told me I could stay with her family for the summer months. She made it clear that her home was always open to me. How I loved her! She was like a mom to me.

"Marilyn," she went on to say with great tenderness, "this is hard for me to say, but I want you to hear something. Even though you feel hurt right now, try to get to the place of honoring your father and your mother."

My first thought was, *How in the world can I honor my dad?* "Joyce, I can't do that!"

"I know it sounds impossible, but, Marilyn, if you don't honor your parents, you will end up with a bitter spirit and that bitterness will destroy not only you but those who are around you. Bitterness is contagious."

She went on to say that I didn't have to honor my dad for the way he treated me but to try to honor him out of respect for his position. She then invited me to come and stay with her for the weekend so we could talk more. She helped me begin to understand that his actions weren't a reflection on me—they were a reflection of his own problems. She had been through similar experiences with our father years before, so she knew what she was talking about.

That first night at my sister's house, my stomach churned. I was so upset with my dad. Over and over he had rejected me. I remembered the times after my mother died that I told him I loved him and hoped he would say he loved me too. As I lay awake in the dark room, I remembered what my dad often said to me whenever I told him I loved him.

"Dad, I love you."

"Yep."

Or sometimes when I told him I loved him, he would remind me of the little story of a husband bird who said to his wife bird, "I love you, I love you." The wife would reply in bird-like, high-sounding chirps, "Then-show-it, then-show-it."

Performance was the way my dad felt loved. He would love me . . . if I cleaned my room . . . if I started dinner before he got home . . . if I took more initiative in life . . . if I remembered to wash out the trash cans with the hose before I brought them back into the garage . . . if I didn't sleep in too long on a Saturday morning. . . . The trouble for me was that no matter how hard I tried, I never felt I performed well enough for him.

"God," I cried out that night my dad told me I could no longer come home, "I don't know what to do. I feel so worthless." That day I had experienced a deep "father wound." My tears fell for a long time on my pillow until they finally quieted my disturbed heart and I fell asleep.

Years later I came across a quote in Augustine's *Confessions*

that brought me back to the despair I felt that night: "The tears
. . . streamed down, and I let them flow as freely as they would,
making of them a pillow for my heart. On them I rested."[2]

My feelings of guilt for not doing what my dad wanted had
gradually begun to change to shame. How did that happen?
Guilt results *from not doing*, but shame results *from not being.* I
not only believed I couldn't do what my dad expected of me,
I believed I wasn't what he wanted in a daughter. *My dad would
let me come home if I was just good enough.*

My dad's rejection added to my feeling less and less confident. Shame in one's life has a way of wiping out self-assurance.
Shameful thinking sounds like this: *If my own father does not want
me, who else would want me? If I can't please my dad, I probably can't
please anyone. There must be something very unlovable about me.* These
and other thoughts take up a growing residence in the vacancy
created by a lack of confidence.

If you feel rejected by your own parents, you, too, are likely
to struggle with bitterness. I believe children's need for their
parents' approval is foundational. Without it, they will have difficulty accepting themselves and approval from anyone else. After
all, if their own parents don't approve of them, who else really
will?

Shame can be spotted in people who always seem to be
angry, as well as those who struggle with a lack of confidence.
Such people have been hurt, which then leads to feelings of
inadequacy. They make up for their lack of confidence by using
anger as a cover-up, a way of looking strong even though they
feel threatened.

Toxic shame also can lead to addictions. People use addictions to try to help numb the pain of shame. When I first heard of this correlation, my immediate thoughts were, *Oh good! I don't have any addictions, so I am not dealing with shame issues.* I read down a list of addictions and patted myself on the back until I came to a certain word. I had no idea it was termed an addiction— *perfectionism!*

I saw that while I had not gone down the anger route with my dad, I had started going down the path of perfectionism, which is another offspring of shame. That, like anger, is an attempt to cover up deep feelings of inferiority. Perfectionism whispers that we will never be able to do anything quite right and that we must try and try again. It seeks to conceal what we feel is unacceptable. Perfectionism is a way to cover up what we hate about ourselves. It is so tiring to have to be perfect.

My negative and perfectionistic thoughts about myself were gradually growing and silently wiping out any of the little self-confidence that remained. I've come to call these negative self-thoughts *shame shapers,* since when they persist, they shape our attitudes and the way we feel about ourselves.

If you tell yourself things like: *No one wants me; I can't please him/her; I'm afraid I'll be a burden,* you are allowing shame to shape you into a person God never intended for you to be. Shame sculpts with dull, rusty knives and then engraves its trademark on you: "worthless."

HOW ABOUT YOU?

1. Do you have any "dislocated relationships"—the kind of relationships that forces you to "do life" with people who continually hurt you? If so, how is it impacting the other areas of your life?

2. Have you experienced a deep father or mother wound that you have not worked through? Are you willing to admit that this hurt exists and then take the necessary steps to begin to clean out the "infection" from this wound?

3. "Lord, when doubts fill my mind, when my heart is in turmoil, quiet me and give me renewed hope and cheer" (Psalm 94:19, TLB). Sometimes we go through a period in life where everything, for quite a while, seems to go wrong—no matter how hard we try. What does Psalm 94:19 tell us about how God can help us handle those times?

4. Have you been able to identify any shame shapers in your life? Shame shapers are experiences that destroyed your confidence or words that negatively impacted how you see yourself. If shame has affected you, how does it come out—as perfectionism, anger, an addiction, or some other self-destructive form?

SHAME Lifters

- If you still struggle because you felt that a parent, friend, spouse, or other important person in your life rejected you, remember this promise in Psalm 27:10 (NLT): "Even if my father and mother abandon me, the LORD will hold me close." Let the truth that God will never abandon or leave you go down deep into your heart. Picture the Lord Jesus with His arms open to receive and hold you.

- If you are part of a new (or even an older) blended family, set up a time with a counselor to talk with your family. Talk about expectations. Set up an appointment for a year later as well. Commit to it like you would for a yearly physical. If your family isn't open to counseling, I strongly urge you to go yourself so you can be emotionally healthy as you deal with your family.

- Seek to speak only positively about family members who are no longer present, whether it be through death or separation. Refuse to listen to slander about those family members or friends. (Note: At times people need to confide in others, discussing hurts that have been inflicted by others. Ask for God's wisdom to know when listening is slanderous and when it is a part of the healing process.)

Dear heavenly Father,

Your Word tells me not to be surprised when I go through various kinds of trials (1 Peter 4:12). This is the way life is here on earth. At times I have experienced deep woundedness by those who cared for me. You understand being wounded. You were wounded for us and by us! Even when You were wounded on the cross Your arms were open to us (Isaiah 53:5).

Thank You for Your promise that You are a shelter for the oppressed and a refuge in times of trouble (Psalm 9:9). I run to You, and You embrace me! Thank You that You long for me, Your child, to come home, knowing that the door is always open (John 17:24). In the healing name of Jesus, Amen.

My Other *Father*

> *"I will be a Father to you, and you will be my sons and daughters," says the Lord Almighty.*
>
> 2 Corinthians 6:18

After spending the entire weekend crying at my sister's house, I returned to my dorm room and tried to settle back into my college routine. Every so often I would think, *I'm an orphan! No one wants me.* My self-pity level continued to rise as I allowed negative shame shapers to do their sculpting work on my thinking. These internal whispers were carving intense feelings of worthlessness and self-disgust into my heart. *If I were just a little bit more creative and outgoing my dad would want me. He is not pleased with me, and I know I am a disappointment to him. There must be lots of things wrong with me if my dad doesn't want me to come home.*

One afternoon a college friend named Barb, who knew I had a difficult relationship with my father, came running into my dorm room.

"Marilyn, I believe God wants you to go to Israel this summer with a study group from college. We'll be going to the Institute of Holy Land Studies located on Mount Zion in Jerusalem.[1] You would be gone for three months, and it would solve the problem of where to live for the summer. Plus, you would receive ten hours of college credit," she said excitedly.

I smiled weakly. "Thanks for trying, Barb, but I need to find housing here and work this summer if I want to come back in the fall." Barb, however, persisted that she "just knew" I was supposed to go to Israel for the summer.

"Barb, there is no way that I have the money for that kind of trip. I can't go!"

"Please, at least go with me to the passport agency and get your passport picture taken. Please!" she insisted.

I finally gave in and laughed all the way there. I had my picture taken but didn't think too much about it after that. It was too big of a dream to even ponder.

A few weeks later I got a call at my dorm from some people I had never met.

"Hi, Marilyn. You don't know us, but we know your sister. She told us about your situation with your dad, and we have a question for you. How would you like to fly to British Columbia, Canada, with our family next weekend? We have some daughters around your age, and we would like to include you in our short weekend family vacation."

I was flabbergasted. After talking with them for a while I said okay. They told me they would have me back in time for my classes on Monday morning.

True to their word, the Bauers included me in their family trip. I had a great time, and it helped to lift some of the depression I felt. As I was getting ready to board the plane to head back to college, Mr. Bauer handed me a check.

"Marilyn, we heard from your sister that you would like to go to Israel this summer. Here is a check for you to go." I had not said a word about Israel to this family.

I glanced down at the check. I had never seen that amount of money before and was shocked. Trying to pull myself together, I thanked Mr. Bauer and somehow stumbled to my seat on the plane.

Heavenly Father, You did this! Thank You! I breathed over and over as I flew back to my college.

At that point I didn't know what I was going to do about a job, but I was so thankful to have a place to *belong* during the summer.

Those three months in Israel were a gift from the Lord. He began to teach me more about transferring my desire for my father's earthly love to my heavenly Father. I began to desire God more than I ever had before. In fact, I became a bit alarmed with these new feelings. I went to one of the pastors in our Israel study group and told him I didn't know what was wrong with me. After he heard my concerns, he smiled a knowing smile. "Marilyn, I know what is wrong with you. You're just hungering and thirsting after God. That's good! Keep hungering for Him, and He will fill you."

More and more I began to experience God's personal love for me. My one and only pair of sandals broke while in Israel. I decided to pray and ask the Lord to somehow supply this need. God put it on the heart of a missionary who was visiting the Institute to buy me a pair of sandals. She had no idea mine were broken. When I asked her how she knew I needed sandals, she replied that she had been praying earlier in the day and sensed the Lord nudging her to offer to buy me a new pair. That amazed me! Looking back, I now recognize times like these as God sightings, just as my mom had taught me to do.

Other students periodically received money in the mail from their parents. I, on the other hand, seemed to receive whatever I needed directly from the Lord—even down to the required exit airport tax. This was an additional fee that we had not been informed about earlier. By the end of our three months I had two pounds in Israeli change left. I found out two days before we left Israel that I needed to pay a twelve-pound exit tax.

I didn't tell anyone that I needed ten more pounds, but instead went to the Lord. "Father, all summer You have cared for me. Now I need ten pounds and I am trusting You for this amount."

The day before we were to leave Israel, I checked my mailbox one more time to see if anyone had sent me any money. It was the Sabbath, so I knew there wouldn't be any mail delivered on that day, but I wanted to check anyway. When I peered through the small glass window on the mailbox, I saw something. As I pulled out and unfolded a piece of notebook paper, a ten-pound note fluttered to the floor. The writing on the paper simply said, "To Marilyn, Love Jesus."

Again, no one knew I had that need! I never found out who put that ten-pound note in my mailbox. As far as I was concerned, however, it was Jesus Himself. It was such a confirmation that the Lord truly was my Father and that He would take care of me. The phrase, "To Marilyn, Love Jesus," stirred my heart as I began to realize that was the way the Father feels about *all* of His children. He does care about us. We are His personal concern! He reveals Himself to us. That ten-pound Israeli note was another God sighting.

After leaving Israel, our group made a stopover in Italy for a few days. We then headed for the Los Angeles International Airport. All the parents were there waiting to welcome us back. All the parents, that is, except mine. I waited quite a while, and since it was getting very late, my friend Barb finally suggested I go home with her for the night. I couldn't reach my parents by phone, so I gratefully agreed. The next day I finally connected with my dad.

"Dad, where were you last night? You told me you would pick me up from the airport and take me to Joyce's house."

"Oh, we completely forgot!"

It was difficult not to feel sorry for myself. In another way, however, it was the same pattern I had experienced with him since I was younger, so it wasn't a big surprise. I guess I had hoped things had changed while I was in Israel. Instead, I realized that my dad still did not want me.

A few days later I stood in the financial aid line at Azusa Pacific. My parents had informed me again that they did not have money to help me with my college bill. I assumed I would not be able to register because I had not worked all summer and had zero money to put down on my college bill.

As I waited, a staff person from the business office came rushing up to me. I braced myself for the bad news I was certain I would receive.

"Marilyn, we just found out that after your mother died she had Social Security money that you never received."

"What are you telling me?" I asked.

"You have Social Security money available to you and it's all retroactive. It will cover your school bill this year, plus give you a little extra spending money," the staff person said excitedly.

I felt as if I had just won a million dollars.

"Are you sure?" I questioned with disbelief.

"Yes!" the financial aid person said, smiling.

It was a dream come true. My heavenly Father had taken care of all my financial needs. Another God sighting!

I began the new semester with a golden tan from my three months in Israel and a new glow of confidence. I thought I had done a good job of pushing away the problems and sadness I had with my dad. I would just have to go on in life as if he didn't exist.

In one of my psychology classes, students were required to take the Taylor-Johnson Temperament Analysis. A few days later my professor, Clinton Jones, whom I highly respected, set up an appointment with me. He wanted to discuss the results of my test.

"Marilyn, I am very concerned about one of your scores," he said gently. "What are you so angry about?"

"Angry? I'm not angry," I replied sincerely.

Professor Jones, an incredibly warm and caring professor, looked me in my eyes and asked, "What is going on in your life?"

It was the first time anyone had ever asked me that question, and I broke down.

"Prof, my dad doesn't love me. He says I may never come home again."

I could see the pain and hurt in his face for my situation and me. After I had poured out my heart, he tenderly shared wise words with me. He reminded me that the root of bitterness has a way of growing in our hearts and can choke the very life out of us. In my case bitterness was causing hidden anger that I had no idea was so close to the surface.

Professor Jones did not want my dad's painful actions to make my heart become hard. The counsel from Professor Jones was a bit of a wake-up call for me. My heart wound was deep, and infectious pus had been accumulating. Only Jesus could reach down deep enough to touch and heal those raw open wounds. Would I let Him? I saw how God had cared for many of my physical needs while I was in Israel and for my financial need when I returned to college, but would I allow Him to care for my unseen, internal needs? Over and over my heavenly Father gently knocked at my heart's door to see if I was ready to allow Him to do a deeper healing in my life.

My appointment with Prof. Jones gave me the opportunity to begin to deal with my bitterness. One way I did this was to start journaling my thoughts to the Lord in a spiral notebook. The journaling helped me to begin to let go of some of the bitterness, hurt, and anger from my dad's rejection. I wrote in my journal that I intended to remain as focused on God as possible for the next six weeks. I relinquished to Jesus my desire to be loved by others, seeking only to love and be loved by Him. I went so far as to turn down all requests for dates during those six weeks! It turned out to be a very healing time.

At the end of those six weeks, I met a wonderful young man named Paul at college. He was one of the best players on the football team and a natural leader. He was also passionate about God and studying to be a pastor. October was Azusa Pacific's homecoming, which included a competitive football game and the crowning of a queen. Much to my surprise, I was nominated for the homecoming court. I was honored but didn't think too much about it. I was only a junior, and three beautiful, well-deserving seniors were also on the court.

On the evening of the homecoming banquet, I stood with the other nominees on a platform and waited for the queen to be announced. "Marilyn is our new queen," the announcer's voice boomed over the PA system. I was overwhelmed as the outgoing queen, Jackie, placed the crown on my head and draped the velvet robe around my shoulders. "Congratulations, Marilyn!" Jackie said with a smile as she handed me a bouquet of long-stemmed red roses.

My brother, Cliff, was finishing up his last year at Azusa Pacific. He came up to me after the banquet with a congratulatory kiss on the cheek.

"Cliff, do you know why Mom and Dad weren't here tonight?"

My brother looked down and quietly said, "Yes, your stepmom had a hair appointment and felt she couldn't change it. I'm sorry, Marilyn. I tried to talk to Dad and Mom about being here tonight."

After the banquet Paul asked if I would drive over to his parents' house with him since they lived only a couple miles from the college. As we walked down the stairs of the banquet area to go to his car I began to cry. Immediately Paul stopped me on the stairs and with great concern said, "Marilyn, what's wrong?"

Could I dare tell him that as I looked over the crowd at the banquet I realized that my dad and stepmom weren't there for me again? And all because of a haircut? While I didn't know I was going to be crowned queen that night, the college administrators did. The students had voted earlier in the day, and the administrators had a policy of calling the parents of the elected queen to invite them to attend the ceremony, especially those who lived close to the college. Since my parents were not far from the college, I wondered why they had not attended.

Finally I blurted out to Paul that I was just disappointed my parents hadn't come. I looked at him and asked, "Why don't they love me?" With a sweet tenderness, Paul took my hand and shaking his head simply said, "I don't know. I don't understand it."

By that time I did *not* look like a newly pronounced homecoming queen. My eyes were puffy from crying and my mascara had smeared, leaving black streaks down my cheeks. I was a mess! When we arrived at Paul's parents' house they greeted me joyously at the front door. They had already heard the news. But once they got a good look at me, they wondered what had happened. Quickly I explained that I had been crying because my parents were not able to make it to the banquet.

"It's silly for me to be so upset about this," I said as I tried to cover up my sadness. "It's just that over and over my parents can't make it to my events, and this time it was because of my mom's hair appointment." Inwardly I thought, *I'm still not good enough for my dad.* Even though the student body at my college had voted for me, I wanted my dad's vote.

Paul's mom put her arms around me and comforted me. She did not minimize my pain or say it was silly for me to be disappointed over such a trivial thing. She knew that pain was pain. She whispered that I was welcome in their home and could go there any time I wanted. "Our home is your home," she told me that night. A bit of solace, comfort, and peace settled over my disappointed heart, and I wiped off the makeup that stained my face.

I kept coming back to the same old question. Why, why, why doesn't my dad love me? Why couldn't I let it go? I kept telling myself, *So what?* So they didn't make it to the homecoming banquet; it was really no big deal. Maybe I should just forget about Dad and get on with life. Why did it matter so much to me? What is it in a person that makes them hunger for an emotionally close parental relationship? I pushed those questions down, hoping that someday things would change.

My life became more wrapped up in Paul after that. It boggled my mind that he wanted to spend time with me. Unlike my father, I could carry on normal conversations with him. Paul was caring, and often I found sweet notes from him in my college mailbox. He also called me frequently. When he asked me to marry him, there was no doubt in my nineteen-year-old heart. I knew I wanted to marry him and said "yes!" with assurance.

Paul and I made a trip to my parents' home, where Paul asked my dad for my hand in marriage. We told them that we planned to marry in July, which would give us an eight-month engagement. When I broke the news to my dad and stepmom, I fully expected them to be relieved, since they didn't seem to want to be involved in my life. They smiled but didn't say too much.

A few months later my dad called me at college and asked if I would come home during my spring break. I couldn't believe my ears! I was being invited back home for a visit for the first time in over fifteen months. I jumped at the opportunity, and Paul offered to drive me to my parents' home and pick me up after spring break. He knew this was important to me.

I did not realize at first that my dad had an agenda. His purpose in inviting me home was to talk me out of marrying

Paul! I was confused. My dad didn't want me, so wouldn't he be glad that I would be someone else's responsibility? My dad would never have to think about caring for me again. For the entire week my dad tried to talk me out of marrying Paul. The reason? He said he was afraid Paul would be "one of those religious liberals."

"Dad, I know where Paul stands with the Lord. He loves Him with all of his heart. I've heard him preach both to the youth group he pastors and also at a couple of Sunday services. He also leads students at a local high school for Youth for Christ. Please, if that's your only concern, please come hear him preach."

No matter how much talking I did, I could not convince my dad. At the end of the spring break week, Paul picked me up to take me back to college.

"How did it go?" Paul asked.

"Not very well," I replied as I looked over at Paul while he was driving. "My dad and stepmom don't want me to marry you. They have worn me down, and I don't know what to do." Poor Paul—he about drove off the road when I told him that.

Thankfully, my mind cleared when I realized that sometimes when you deal with a person who can be difficult it can get quite confusing and crazy! I called my dad and told him that I *was* going to marry Paul and that if he wanted he could hear him preach. My dad eventually did drive out to hear Paul. Afterward my dad made one of the most meaningful statements to me: "I'll not worry about you being with him anymore."

With that green light from my dad and the wedding date approaching, I decided to ask my parents if they could help with any of the wedding expenses.

"We're sorry, Marilyn, but we can't afford to pay for a wedding." *Here I go again. Why did I even ask them for help? I know better.* The feelings of being a burden intensified. I crumpled inside again with discouragement. *Heavenly Father, would You please help me? You have, over and over, provided and cared for my needs. This is a big request to ask You—to help me cover the costs of a wedding. I have no idea how this will all work out, but I know You will help me somehow. Thank you, Father.*

My sister, Joyce, had been helping me secure a photographer, book the church and organist, and handle many other details. She knew I didn't have money to cover the wedding costs, so she went to talk to our dad. She was upset when he told her the same thing he told me—no money.

Amazingly, the Bauer family, who had paid for my trip to Israel, called my sister to check on the financial status of my wedding. They had been concerned for me and were even seriously considering officially adopting me right before I met Paul. When Joyce told them that my parents were not able to help with wedding expenses, they called me.

"Marilyn, we understand that your dad is not able to pay for your wedding. We want to pay for the entire wedding, so just let us know how much you need. We want you to have the wedding of your dreams. We've also planned a trip to a ranch in Montana a month after your wedding and we want you and Paul to join us—all expenses paid."

I was amazed! It truly felt like a dream come true, and it was definitely yet another God sighting.

I remember, as a bride, walking down the aisle that July afternoon thinking, *Mother, I wish you were here today.* Almost as if on cue, I had a sense of her being there. Whether or not it was real didn't matter. I felt as if she was there for me. Also, I will never forget the look on Paul's face as I walked toward him. He was smiling. Oh, to feel so cherished and wanted!

Often the first year of marriage is a bit difficult—lots of ups and downs as two people seek to adjust their lives together to become one. Our first year of marriage, however, was incredible to me. Each day I woke up hardly daring to believe that someone like Paul loved me and didn't expect me to be perfect. It seemed too good to be true. I didn't realize at the time that I had been a shame receiver for many years before I married Paul. Had I known that, I would have understood that shame receivers will hear and receive bad things said about them but will let *any good or positive* comments bounce off of them. While Paul was good about affirming me, my old pattern of thinking continually made me wonder how he could love me.

We settled into married life and saw my dad and stepmom only occasionally. Weekends were busy for all of us. My dad was pastoring a church, and Paul, a youth pastor, and I were serving a church in another city.

Even though things were going well, something deep inside me still longed to be wanted and loved by my dad. In fact, now that I was married, I thought my dad would respect me more as an adult—particularly since he no longer had any responsibility for me. My expectations would build to such a point that I actually believed the next time I saw my dad he would have changed. But my hopes were dashed over and over. By age thirty I finally began to accept that my dad wasn't going to change. It hit me hard one day . . . I could not change or fix my dad! After fifteen years of consciously trying to please and perform for my dad, I realized that nothing had happened. Perhaps I would have to be the one to change, but how?

I poured out my heart to the Lord—again. *Father, I have wanted a father's love for so long. I keep coming back to this problem. How do I truly give it up to You? Please show me what to do.*

By this time we had moved from California to Michigan, where my husband had accepted a senior pastor position. Soon after I met Joy, who was also a pastor's wife. I told her a bit about the struggle I was having with my dad, as well as my own feelings of inadequacy about being a pastor's wife. She challenged me to begin making time to be in God's Word on a daily basis. I quietly laughed at her suggestion. How would that solve my situation? *There is nothing in Scripture about a daughter wanting her father's love*, I thought to myself.

"Marilyn," Joy continued, "read God's Word until He speaks to you. And journal what you sense the Lord is speaking to you from your reading."

She told me I would find strength for each day as I read the Bible. A little unsure at first, I took her up on her suggestion. It was wonderful how it seemed to perk me up when I was down, or how it spoke to whatever was going on in my day. Little by little I began to understand the importance of reading God's Word on a *daily* basis and waiting to hear what He wanted to say to me.[2]

One day I was reading from the Old Testament book of Nehemiah and came across a passage where Nehemiah tells the Lord all the things he had done for the people of Israel while he had been helping to repair the city walls of Jerusalem. I laughed out loud.

"Father, do You know what Nehemiah wanted from You? He wanted affirmation!" I said.

Quietly but clearly I heard these words in my mind: *Yes, Marilyn, and that is exactly what you want from your dad— affirmation. You are not going to get that from him, but if you come to Me I will affirm you.*

I began weeping because those words hit the core of my woundedness. I had an *inattentive* earthly father. But I also had a deeply caring, fully *attentive* heavenly Father who pays attention to the needs of His children.

Oh, Father, I do want his affirmation so badly. Every time I talk to

*my dad I always hope he will change. He never does. I understand that
I cannot fix my dad, Lord Jesus. Even though my dad may not be able
to change, I can change with Your help.*

I can't explain exactly what happened to me in those
moments, but something changed. Even though that passage
of Scripture from Nehemiah never mentioned anything about
forgiveness or about a father-daughter relationship, the Lord
used His Word to cleanse and heal my infected heart! I *wanted* to
forgive my dad. It was as if the Lord was placing a choice before
me to either forgive or not forgive. I was tired of holding on to
the inability to forgive that was wearing me down, and I was
tired of waiting for my dad to affirm me.

"Father, I forgive my dad," I said aloud. Forgiveness began
to wash over me as I released my dad from my complaints of
neglect, emotional abuse, and abandonment. It was as if God,
at that moment, was literally extracting the root of bitterness
from my heart. And instead of leaving a big gaping hole, the
Lord Jesus filled it with the sweetness of His compassion. He
exchanged my bitterness for His compassion! There was no way
I could have done that on my own. All of a sudden my dad was
a different person to me. I felt a genuine compassion and love
for him. My soul felt engulfed in God's peace and grace. It was
to be the beginning of the Lord taking the sting out of my sad
memories. I no longer felt the compulsion to try to please my
dad. And I had also been released from my unmet longings of
wanting my dad to please and affirm me.

During this time of healing, I was to learn more about bitterness. Bitterness is a sign of an unhealed heart. Bitterness puts
you into an "emotional stuck point" as you rehearse offenses

over and over. Its symptoms include low-grade anger, prolonged depression, and resentment. After a while, you begin to justify your bitterness, which paves the way to developing a deep-seated grudge. Sadly, bitterness closes off a part of your heart to God so that He cannot have full access to you and your pain. Your heart becomes brittle. Bitterness eventually destroys *you*, not the one who wounded you!

I began to picture the bitterness I had felt toward my dad as a set of handcuffs. I had one handcuff clasped on my wrist and the other one clasped on my dad's wrist. Every day I had walked through life dragging my dad around with me. (Obviously he had no idea.) It was a heavy weight to bear, and I was only hurting myself. There was such joy in releasing him from that handcuff once I realized it.

My friend Danae offers another helpful visual of bitterness. Picture yourself walking in a crowded room carrying a cup of very hot coffee with no lid. All of a sudden someone bumps into you. What sloshes out? Hot coffee. Now picture *yourself as a cup* with no lid. As people "bump" into you in life, what comes out of you? If it is bitterness, it will spill out and burn you as well as others. Scripture wisely admonishes us to "watch out that no bitterness takes root among you, for as it springs up it causes deep trouble, hurting many in their spiritual lives" (Hebrews 12:15, TLB).

The antidote to bitterness, as difficult as it can be, is to take your eyes off the one who has hurt you and focus them on God. In fact, that's just what Jesus did: "Let us fix our eyes on Jesus, the author and perfecter of our faith, who for the joy set before him endured the cross, *scorning its shame*, and sat down at the right hand of the throne of God" (Hebrews 12:2, italics added). Did you catch that? Even Jesus had to fix His eyes above when faced with shame. He looked forward to the joy that awaited Him after He endured the cross. He didn't allow Himself to become bitter—although He had every right to feel that way toward the religious leaders. He took His eyes off His abusers and saw His father waiting for Him with joyous, welcoming arms.

One way that you can focus on God is by actively looking for the positive ways He has been working in *your* life (what I've been calling God sightings), both now and in past painful events. Allow yourself to replay memories and look for God in them. When you do this, you'll begin to realize that He is there *with* you now and has always been with you. He sees the hurt the other person has caused you. Recognizing that God has been working in your past and is working in your present will help to destroy the tenacious root of bitterness. With God's help, you'll be able to release the "handcuffs" that bind you to the person who has caused you such pain.

When I think back to my college days, I remember the Bauers. As a shamed person, I felt very exposed. The Bauers "covered" (protected) me emotionally and financially, which helped me move forward. Not only did they pay for my Israel trip and wedding, they helped me get perspective on my situation. They told me over and over that most fathers wouldn't respond to their children as my father had done to me. They showed their concern every time he did not act like a father should. The Bauers were grace-filled people who extended grace to me. Looking back, it was God working through them during my difficult time.

Another key to releasing bitterness is filling your mind and heart with God's Word. When I began dealing with my own bitterness as a young adult, I knew the Bible was a great book. However, I'd never experienced the power of its God-breathed, living, and active words. Only when I personally encountered this living Word did I realize it wasn't just a book of platitudes. What other book is able to judge our thoughts and reveal our attitudes? Reading God's Word does four things for each of us: it *teaches, rebukes, corrects,* and *trains* us in righteousness so that we're ready and equipped for every good work (see 2 Timothy 3:16-17).

The Bible is a tool that will help each of us clarify our struggles against bitterness and other vices. My husband gave me this helpful illustration to show how the Spirit of God can work through His Word to touch our lives. Picture an iceberg. Above the waterline you see the top of an iceberg. What you don't see is all of the ice below the waterline. Scientists estimate that approximately only one-ninth of every iceberg, no matter its size, is above the water. Almost all of it is submerged in water. And, of course, it's what we can't see that can cause the most problems. The same is true of the contents of our hearts. We often know the issues that we are dealing with *above* the water-line. It's those other issues, deep down, that we may not even be fully aware of that God would like to reach. Thankfully, as we read His Word and pray for God's discernment, the Lord lowers the waterline and asks, *What about this? Are you willing for Me to reveal more of what's really there?* If we are, He kindly points out issues that need to be identified, worked on, and healed.

Actively looking for the way God has been at work in our lives and listening for His voice in the Bible will help us see that God was there for us even in very dark times. This I know for sure: forgiving and releasing bitterness made it easier to deal with my dad.

After that afternoon when I forgave my father, I felt I had changed. Yet I knew there was a physical buffer of 2,500 miles separating us. What would happen the next time I was *with*

my dad? Would this forgiveness hold even when we were together? Was it for real? Would my feelings of bitterness, resentment, grudges, and fears still be gone when I actually saw him face-to-face?

HOW ABOUT YOU?

1. Is there someone in your life you continually hope will change, only to find that your hopes are dashed again and again? How difficult is it for you to accept that you cannot "fix" him or her and that it's possible this person will not change?

2. Remember how the Lord provided the exit tax I needed to leave Israel? Put your name in the phrase: "To _____, Love Jesus." What do you think the Lord Jesus wants to give to *you* right now?

3. Look back on your life and identify at least one God sighting.

4. Job 21:23-25 points out that "one man dies in full vigor, completely secure and at ease, his body well nourished, his bones rich with marrow. Another man dies in *bitterness of soul*, never having enjoyed anything good" (italics mine). Do you carry any symptoms of bitterness? If so, is it manifested in anger, resentment, negativity? When people "bump" into you, what spills out of you?

5. Affirmation was one of my deepest—yet unnamed—soul needs for many years. What area "below the waterline" do you need God to reveal and then help you work through? It may be helpful to draw an iceberg. Write down issues you already have an awareness of on the top portion of the iceberg. Next, ask the Lord to reveal any issues that may exist below the waterline. If something comes to mind, write it down below the waterline. What would it take for you to move that issue to the top of the iceberg as an acknowledgment that you are seeking to work on that issue as well?

6. Is there a person in your life whom you find difficult to be around or deal with? Jesus understands. He had to deal with difficult religious leaders. Scripture also mentions that His own brothers did not believe in Him (before His resurrection). Check out John 7:3-4 for what they said to Jesus. Can you relate in any way?

7. Can you think of anyone who has been like the Bauer family to you? Are you able to be a "Bauer" to someone you know who is hurting or needs financial help?

❋ ❋ SHAME *Lifters* ❋ ❋

- Identify a family member, friend, or coworker who could use some affirmation. Write down his or her name and make it a point to intentionally affirm that person. Keep in mind that it takes fifteen positive comments to override one negative comment!
- The next time your spouse or child calls you on the phone,

stop and pay attention to the way you greet him or her. Does your voice communicate that you're glad he or she called or does it convey a dull, "Hello, not you again" response? People can "hear" a smile in your voice over the phone. As I'm writing this I just heard my husband call his mom on his cell phone. Even from where I am sitting I could hear her laughter and joyous response on her end of the line when she found out it was her son. Talk about being affirmed!

- Send an anonymous gift to someone you know who is struggling financially. Even if you can only afford to give five dollars, ask God to direct your resources to someone in need.
- Look back on the last month and reinterpret any "coincidences" as God's divine intervention in your life. List some of those God sightings. Thank Him for His presence.

Dear heavenly Father,

Thank You for the way You are always there for me even when I don't see You at work. You are always working—that includes my past, present, and future. Help me to catch glimpses of You more and more in my day and to recognize these God sightings (Psalm 66:5).

Help me to be open to Your divine scrutiny (Psalm 139:23). You see things in me that I do not see. You see below my waterline and desire to help me as I allow You to work in my life. You not only forgive me for hurting You (Psalm 103:10), You also help me extend forgiveness to those who have hurt me (Ephesians 4:32).

I invite You to pull out any roots of bitterness in my life and exchange them for Your peace and compassion (Hebrews 12:15). I realize I cannot fix or change people, but I am giving You permission to change me!

Thank You that You are never inattentive to my needs. Your thoughts are always turned toward me (Psalm 139:17, NLT). Thank You for being an attentive God. In Your powerful name, Amen.

SEVEN

Seeing the "Give" in Forgiveness

*Broken soil brings wheat,
broken clouds bring rain,
broken bread brings strength,
and a broken person is what God
chooses to use for His purposes.*

—Brad Johnson

I finally saw my dad two years after I had determined to forgive him and release my bitterness toward him. My father had called me from California with two requests: "Marilyn, my brother David died. Could I fly out to Michigan and stay with you while I attend the funeral? I was named the sole executor of my brother's estate and there will be lots of things to go through. Could you also help me do an estate sale?"

"Of course, Dad, we'd be glad to have you stay with us. And I'd be able to help you with the estate sale," I responded. Inwardly, however, I had a mix of emotions ranging from surprise to caution to hope. This was going to be a test. Would the forgiveness still be there after two years?

"Is Elizabeth coming too?" I asked.

"No, Elizabeth isn't much into flying."

"Okay, Dad. We'll see you in a couple of days. Good-bye."

I felt a twinge of hurt when I heard that my stepmom was

not flying out. Was unforgiveness going to show its ugly head again? We had lived in Michigan for six years, and she and my dad had never visited us. We had made occasional trips back to California to see my in-laws and my parents, but they did not come out to see us. (In fact, my stepmom never did visit.)

My dad arrived, and he was my same old dad. He'd get irritated and impatient with our young children for the smallest things. If someone rang the doorbell, all three of our children would run to the door, waiting for me to open it.

"Marilyn, why do all the kids have to run to the door every time the doorbell rings? That bothers me."

"Dad, they're just curious, that's all."

In an attempt to help my dad get to know his grandchildren, I decided to take him out to lunch with our youngest daughter, Mandy. The other two children were in school, and Mandy was a sweet and compliant three-year-old. We ordered our lunches, and while we were waiting for them to arrive, Mandy accidentally spilled her water on her pink giraffe overalls. It was really no big deal, but my dad flew into a tizzy. He berated her for her clumsiness and went on and on, saying to her, "Look what you've done!"

"Dad, it's okay," I kept repeating calmly. "It's only water; it will dry. She didn't do it on purpose."

My heart broke for little Mandy. She was obviously frightened of her grandpa. It reminded me of the many times I had spilled my milk. It also reminded me of how I had once feared my dad's words. Though I was a bit annoyed at my dad, I also felt sorry for him. He could not see that he was overreacting and didn't know how to be tender to a little girl who'd made a childish mistake.

The next morning I brought back our garbage cans from the curbside. My dad was frustrated that I had not washed out the cans with the hose before I placed them back in the garage. After she witnessed the trash can scene, my oldest daughter, Christy, asked, "Why is Grandpa mean?"

So many things bothered him. The old me would have reacted and tried to please him. I probably would have gone right out and washed the trash cans. However, I was able to distance myself from his frustration and instead feel compassion for my father. He was so wounded.

During my dad's visit, my first published magazine article arrived in the mail. "Look, Dad, here's my first published article. I just found out that *Christian Reader* magazine has also picked it up."

My dad took a quick glance at the magazine I was holding and said, "Uh-huh."

He then went on to say, "Did I tell you I have been writing lots of poems and they are going to be published?"

"No, Dad, I didn't know that. That's good news for you. Who is publishing them?"

"Oh, you know the publishing companies that offer to print your poems in a book with other people's poems?"

"Yes," I replied.

"Well, for a small fee they will print mine, and it will come out in a nice leather-bound book."

For a moment I was silent. I waited to feel frustrated that my dad couldn't affirm my very first magazine article. I waited to see if I would react to him for changing the subject to focus on himself. I had hoped he would respond, "Marilyn, I am really proud of your magazine article. What an accomplishment. How special that you were asked to write this and then another magazine bought it as well." I also wished he had chosen another time to tell me about *his* writing.

Yet I did not feel frustrated with him, even though he never read my article. A sweet sadness swept over me for my dad. He had such a hard time hearing about someone else's accomplishments without talking about his. The Lord seemed to whisper, *This is not about you, it's about your father.* My dad wanted affirmation!

My dad finished up the business matters with his brother's estate and flew back to California. He had not changed, but one thing was certain: I had. I could now look at him in a different light. I saw how needy he was, and my heart filled with even more compassion and love for him. The Lord also showed me that forgiveness involves much humility and dying to self. I had to *choose* to let go of some things that bothered me. It was an opportunity to *try* to live out Ephesians 4:2: "Be humble and gentle. Be patient with each other, making allowance for each other's faults because of your love" (NLT).

I also saw my dad as someone who was not healthy, which made it easier for me to make allowances for him. I still longed for him to tell me he loved me, but I knew that would possibly never happen and I had to accept that. The forgiveness for my dad that had washed over me two years prior to his visit was real. Forgiveness and compassion had held me together during his stay with us. Instead of harboring feelings of frustration and craziness toward my dad, I felt a calm and peaceful spirit.

My dad called me after he arrived home from his flight.

"Hello, Marilyn. I just wanted to say . . ." There was a lengthy pause as my dad searched for words. "Uh, uh . . ." I continued to wait as he had difficulty putting his thoughts into words. Finally with halting words he said something I will never forget: "Thank you for letting me stay in your home. It was the best time I ever had with you and . . ."—another long pause—"I love you dearly."

I almost dropped the phone. I was thirty-two years old and had just heard my dad tell me he loved me. It was a miracle!

As wonderful as it was to hear my dad's words, the real miracle was that I was able to reply sincerely to my father, "And, Daddy, I love you." I truly felt it and meant it. Forgiveness was real, and I found it to be a positive, powerful force in my life. As difficult as it is to forgive someone, it is so freeing to do so!

After that phone call with my dad, I admit I had high hopes for more of those kinds of conversations. That was not to be the case. It proved to me again, however, that while my dad hadn't changed, the Lord was continuing His healing work of grace in my life. This forgiveness thing wasn't just some temporary emotional high, it was real. God continued to renew my hope that He would fill the needs my earthly father could never meet.

A few years later I learned that my dad had had a stroke and was close to death. I flew out to California and visited him in a nursing home.

I stood by his bedside and took his hand.

"Marilyn, I want to go home."

"I know, Daddy, but you have to stay here for right now."

"Please, I want to go home," he pleaded.

My heart broke for him as I tried to explain that Elizabeth was not physically able to care for him and to give him the medical help he needed after his stroke. He needed people to help lift him and to turn him over in his bed.

His blue eyes searched mine. "I want to go home—to heaven."

Tears came down my cheeks. "I'm sorry, Dad, it's your heavenly home that you are longing for, isn't it?"

"Yes."

For the first time I felt as if I was the parent and he was the child. Our roles were reversed. He clung to my hand as he searched my face to see if I could grant him his wish to leave the nursing home.

All I could do was stay by his bedside and sing some of his favorite hymns. During that time he looked at me and said he wanted to tell me something. Knowing they would probably be some of the last words I would hear from him, I listened carefully.

"Marilyn," he whispered, "I planted six churches in my lifetime, but I lost my own family." I quietly gasped. My heart, again, melted in compassion for him as tears formed in my eyes. I had never heard my dad speak of his negligence of his family. I had never heard him be so transparent. He could have stopped there with his admission, and it would have been enough. But he had more to say.

"You and Paul are in a church ministry. Don't ever get so busy that you neglect your family. Do you hear me?" He kept his blue eyes steadily focused on me until he knew I got his message.

I nodded my head and tried to swallow the lump that was forming in my throat. "Paul and I are really trying to make time for our children. Thanks for your advice, Dad."

Satisfied that I heard him on that account, he went on. "Do you remember me telling you that when I was nine my father died?"

"Yes, Dad, I remember the story."

"But did I tell you that when my aunt came to pick me up from school to tell me of my father's death I started to cry?"

"No," I replied as I leaned in closer to him. "What happened next?"

"When my aunt heard me crying she slapped me across the face and said, 'Be quiet; don't cry!'"

My heart sank for my dad. It hit me hard—my dad had grown up believing crying was a weakness! No wonder my crying did not sit well with my father. He was simply passing on what he had been taught. He never got rid of his "old baggage," and so he tried to enlist his children to help carry it.

My dad was quiet for a few moments and then continued. "There's one other thing I want to tell you."

"Yes, Dad, I'm listening."

"My . . . my brother," he stammered, "physically hurt me when we were younger. He hurt me in my 'private place.'" My dad was tremendously embarrassed to share that last bit of information with me, but it seemed to bring some relief to his troubled thoughts. His shameful secret was out.

I hardly knew how to respond to him at first. Here was my eighty-two-year-old dad sharing a painful secret. His openness, however, not only intensified my compassion level but it also served to endear him to me even more. "Oh Dad, I am so sorry for you! That was a terrible thing for you to go through. Thank you for telling me," I said as we wept together.

My dad died shortly after that. Ironically, that last conversation was the best talk I had ever had with him. He was authentic and transparent, and our conversation partly revealed why my dad responded to his children as he did. He had been hurt in life. As author Sandra D. Wilson puts it in one of her book titles, "Hurt people hurt people."[1] My father, like a wounded animal, hurt those around him, but he had no idea what he was doing. He acted out of self-defense, preservation, and shame.

I found my dad's funeral to be a puzzling experience. I was grateful for the last conversation we had together, but why didn't I feel the same grief and sadness I felt when my mom died? Why were there so few tears? I felt guilty for not feeling more sorrow. Then I realized that the closer you are emotionally with a person, the stronger the grieving when they die. The opposite is true as well. My dad and I had never built our relationship on a healthy emotional foundation. I grieved for what we never had but could have had. I still had a hard time figuring out my dad until my brother told me something that was helpful to me.

A couple of years before my father's death, my brother had taken my dad to have various tests done at a medical center. The test scores showed that his intelligence was literally at a genius level. The medical doctor explained that while my dad was very intelligent, he had a hard time relating to people, particularly his children.

Now my dad was gone. I could no longer try to relate to or understand him. No longer would his words or actions negatively impact me. Or would they?

Even though I had forgiven my dad and our relationship had slightly improved before he died, I realized I had kept his shame-based words alive in my heart. Unintentionally, I still believed the old tapes that played in my head—even though my dad was not saying those things to me anymore. I kept recycling the same lies in my thoughts: *I'm not quite good enough; I don't measure up; Be careful not to be a burden to people; Don't ask for help.* I was the one perpetuating those thoughts—*not my dad!* Shame is an ongoing self-deficiency disease. I kept failing to meet the high expectations I had of myself.

I remember talking to my sister about our dad one day.

"Joyce, I feel fearful that one day I will be just like Dad."

She smiled and said, "Honey, I know that won't happen to you."

"How do you know that, Joyce?"

"First of all, I see only the good traits from Dad in you—not his weak areas. Also, the fact that you are conscious of not wanting to be like our father will keep you from making some of the same mistakes he did. But I should also tell you that if you continue to focus only on how much you don't want to be like Dad, it is possible you *will* become just like him."

She talked to me further, and I came away with two conclusions. I needed to continue to ask our heavenly Father to help me be the person He wanted me to be and, in fact, the person He *already* saw me to be. Next, it would be important for me to keep my eyes fixed on Jesus. After all, He is the Author in our life, and we are complete in Him.

Years after that conversation, our oldest daughter, Christy, was graduating from high school. She and I went to the store and had fun buying all the things she would need for her college dorm. We plopped everything down on our kitchen floor and looked at the huge pile of stuff. One minute we were laughing, but the next minute tears came to my eyes.

"Mom, what's wrong?" Christy asked with concern. "Are you sad I'm leaving for college in a couple of weeks?"

"Well, yes, I know I am going to miss you terribly, but it's more of a bittersweet feeling. I'm so happy for you to be able to go to college, yet sad because we will miss you at home. But I realized something else as I looked at this pile of stuff on the kitchen floor."

"What's that, Mom?"

"It just hit me that I never had a mom or dad who helped me get ready for college."

For a moment I was again caught up in my lonely memories of going off to college with no parents and no money. Earlier in the day I had read that sometimes the Lord allows a painful memory to surface. The memory He had just brought to my mind, however, was *not* intended to cause pain but was brought up for *learning* and *blessing*.

Silently I asked the Lord, *Okay, Lord, what did I learn from this memory?* As quickly as I asked the question there was a quiet answer: *You can be the parent you never had.* I quickly grabbed a pen and wrote that statement down.

And, Father, I continued, *what is the blessing of having that memory resurface again?*

Once again the same still voice penetrated my thoughts and heart: *You have reacted and responded in the way a parent should respond to a child leaving for college—Marilyn, you broke the cycle—it wasn't repeated!*

Those words were powerful, and I knew it was truth coming from the inner depths of my soul. I jotted those words down on the paper as well and pondered them for a long while.

I wasn't like my dad. I was different; I was me! I wasn't repeating the things he had done or not done for me. It was so freeing to realize that. The fear of becoming like him melted away. God was showing me He wanted me to work on becoming more like my heavenly Father.

When I first extended genuine forgiveness to my dad, I thought I had come to the end of a long journey. Little did I realize the journey would continue for many years. (I now compare the journey of forgiveness to childbirth. It can be a painful, often drawn-out process, but it's worth it in the end!) The healing of a heart usually takes a while, and God desired to take me to an even deeper level of healing.

Just as I had to peel off leaf after leaf on an artichoke, there were many more layers of leaves to be peeled away to get to the innermost part of my heart. God could see, even underneath all those layers, the secret, shameful issue I had tucked away when I was a little girl years before. It would still be some time before that leaf was peeled away.

As my father opened up to me in the last few days of his life, I learned some interesting things about shame. When people experience deep shame, they pass it on. Why? To make up for the inadequacies they feel inside themselves, they seek power and control over others. For example, my dad was shamed and punished as a nine-year-old boy for crying about his father's death. He concluded that crying was a weakness. Since he learned that crying should not be tolerated, I believe he shamed anyone else who reminded him of this weakness. Once he shamed a person, he was satisfied that he had done his duty. It gave him a sense of power over the shame he felt, and it put him in control. And yet because he had never dealt with his own shame, he passed it down to me. That's why the time with Christy in our kitchen was such a big deal. I saw for the first time that shame could be stopped. Our children did not have to carry my baggage of shame. The same is true for you and your situation.

Shortly after I realized I had broken the cycle, my family and I flew to California to visit my stepmom. We had a good visit and were just packing up to leave when she asked me to go into the garage with her.

"Marilyn, come here. I want to give you something." She led me to some boxes stacked along the garage wall. She opened a box and pulled out a ruby red and clear glass luncheon plate.

"My mother's King's Crown dishes!" I exclaimed.

"Here, I want you to have them. They are yours now."

I was stunned. These were the very dishes we had washed together many years before. These were the dishes I had vowed never to mention again.

Tears stung my eyes. As I looked from the box of dishes to my stepmom, I noticed she was crying too. She knew! She remembered! While she didn't communicate it in words, she was making an attempt through her physical actions to reconcile us as stepmom and stepdaughter. She was living out Romans 12:18: "If it is possible, as far as it depends on you, live at peace with everyone." We embraced for a long time, not saying a word. Forgiveness was doing its powerful, cleansing work—again.

The dishes were beautiful, and I was very excited to have them. They were extremely valuable to me. I knew one day I wanted to pass them down to my children as a keepsake. But then it hit me. If I had not forgiven my stepmom, I would have passed down the inheritance of a bitter spirit to my children—the next generation.

I wanted my children to know that God uses broken people. People who are broken and contrite in spirit are what God desires more than anything. He knows that proud people will not seek or even try to give forgiveness. What would have happened if my stepmom had remained proud and not shared those dishes with me? What would have happened if I had been proud and not accepted her peace offering?

The joy of knowing that *forgiveness* had changed my inheritance plan caught my breath. These dishes would no longer remind me of something that had been taken away from me, but of the healing balm that happened when two people said they were sorry. Those dishes have the word *forgiveness* written all over them, and they always will.

There's a word within the word *forgiveness* that really struck me when I first noticed it. It's right in the middle of the word— *give*. Forgiveness requires one to give, even if the other person doesn't reciprocate. To give up the hurt you want so badly to hang on to. To give up the right to make the other person pay for what he or she did. To give up a bad attitude about the person who hurt you. To give up bad-mouthing the person who crushed you. Give, give, give—forgive!

Oh, how difficult for*give*ness can be, but how freeing it is. As

C. H. Spurgeon said: "To *be forgiven* is such sweetness that honey is tasteless in comparison with it. But yet there is one thing sweeter still and that is *to forgive*."[2]

HOW ABOUT YOU?

1. Three phrases are sometimes difficult for us to say: "I'm sorry"; "I forgive you"; and "I love you." Is there anyone you would like to hear any of those phrases from? Is there someone you need to say any of those phrases to?

2. Have your parents ever shared some of their past with you? How did their words help you understand where they were coming from? In what ways, if any, has their baggage affected your adult life?

3. Do you catch yourself repeating negative statements you heard from people years ago? Are you passing on the disease of shame to the next generation in any way?

4. What specific destructive cycles has God already helped you break? Celebrate that and rejoice! What other cycles still need to be broken?

5. Look back at the quote from Brad Johnson at the beginning of this chapter. Do you consider yourself a "broken" person? How might God use your brokenness to help others?

6. Have you ever noticed the word *give* in the word *forgiveness*? What significance does that have when you consider offering forgiveness to someone who doesn't deserve it?

※　　※　SHAME *Lifters*　※　　※

- Everybody carries baggage into life. Take a moment and allow yourself to look into your own "suitcase." What do you see? Are there any pieces of resentment, containers of bitterness, boxed-up worries and fears, or folded-up regrets? Perhaps you'll find something else stuffed into a zippered pocket of your luggage as well. By allowing yourself to look inside, you can begin to recognize any excess baggage you may be carrying. You'll also be in the position to begin unpacking and tossing out the extra weight you carry. Another benefit of recognizing and dealing with your excess baggage is this: others will not have to carry it for you. You will have stopped the generational baggage from going further!
- Tell one family member or friend today that you love him or her. Don't just say a quick "love ya." Look that person in the eyes and use an "I" statement. Say something like "I've been meaning to tell you that I really love and admire you!"
- If your parents or grandparents are still living, what could you say or do that would help them in this season of life? Seek to

honor them (whether you think they deserve it or not) with a phone call, visit, or card this week.

Dear heavenly Father,

How amazing that while You were on the cross You wanted to give us the gift of forgiveness even though we did not deserve it (Luke 23:34). What a costly gift! Help me to be like You and offer forgiveness to those around me (Colossians 3:13). You know that it is often hard for me to do that and yet You stand ready to help me.

Thank You that no matter what someone else may have done to me, with Your help, I can break that awful cycle. I don't have to repeat what was done to me (Philippians 4:13). Help me to leave my loved ones a joyous spiritual inheritance instead of a bitter legacy (Proverbs 10:7). In Your powerful and cycle-breaking name, Amen.

EIGHT

Forgive and *Reforgive*

When Jesus took on the weight of your sin and carried
it to the cross, He also carried the sins committed against
you. When you insist on holding on to the hurts inflicted
on you, you deny the power of His crucifixion.
—Jennifer Kennedy Dean, *He Leads Me Beside Still Waters*

My family and I flew home from California with the box of
King's Crown dishes on my lap. I felt as if a part of my mother
was going home with me. I was also taking home a part of
my heart that had been healed. How wonderful that the Lord
allowed this reconciliation to happen before my stepmom passed
away several years later.

The Lord continued to wait patiently to work in other areas
of my heart as well. He knew I still had the door of that secret,
shameful memory locked tightly in my heart's closet. I could not
and would not give Him access. It was on a foolproof security
system. He would wait with me on that one. . . .

In the meantime, my husband and I found ourselves flying
out to California again, this time for a leadership conference in
Carmel on the coastline of the Pacific Ocean. I had several days
of uninterrupted solitude, which gave me time to think and
journal my thoughts.

We decided to conclude our time in Carmel by renting a car and driving to see Paul's parents. As we took the freeway to their home, something happened to me as I began to see exit signs for the places where I grew up. I had not been back to my hometown in many years. It was strange seeing familiar signs again. After a while I saw a sign that read "To Barstow." Immediately something inside of me snapped. It was on the way to Barstow that my dad had left me along the side of the road when I was five.

I was angry! Where had that anger come from? Why did that memory emerge again, and this time with such vehemence? What was going on? I had forgiven my dad for that incident a long time ago.

I told Paul about the emotions I was going through as we drove.

"Paul, how could a parent drop off a small child along the road?" I asked, horrified.

"I don't know; it sure makes you wonder what was going on in his head when he did that," Paul said sadly, shaking his head.

"I don't think any parent in their right mind would do such a thing! We never did that to our kids, and we had plenty of crying times in the car with our five children! Why did my dad do that?"

For the first time, I was really angry about that memory. I was baffled for a moment, however, as to where that intense anger had bubbled up from. I also felt guilty for being angry over a memory I was sure I had already forgiven. Then I realized that years before I had pushed that anger way down and pretended it wasn't there.

We arrived at my in-laws' house, and after dinner I knew I needed to take another look at my anger. Obviously the Lord had lowered the waterline on my life and wanted to show me something.

Father, I called out from the guest room, *I have so many* questions. *How could my dad leave me like that? What made him do that? Why am I dealing with this anger and this memory again?*

Marilyn, sometimes a wound is reopened for a deeper, stronger, and even more powerful healing.

I didn't realize that the wound needed to be reopened.

What do you see in that memory, My child?

I made myself go back and look again at that memory.

Father, I see a little girl standing on the shoulder of the road with her little suitcase next to her. Her back is to me.

Now I want you to look again, My child.

Hesitantly I allowed myself to face the scene of that memory one more time. This time I reimagined the scene with Christ in it. As I looked, I saw something I had not seen the first time.

Father, I still see the little girl standing on the shoulder of the road with her back to me and her little suitcase next to her. But, Father, this time I see the form of Jesus standing with the little girl holding her right hand! My breath caught as this realization hit me. *Jesus was with me all the time, wasn't He?* I asked incredulously.

Yes, My child. I never left you and have never abandoned you. I did not leave you along the road; your father did. I cried with you. I was there for you.

I realized then that God was allowing my anger to come to the surface—not as an enemy, but as *a friend.* My newly unearthed anger was forcing me to gain a deeper understanding and healing of the wound. I would have missed this beautiful image of Jesus had I kept my anger stuffed down inside.

God also reminded me of the verse I had read and journaled about that very morning. I quickly got out my Bible to read the verse again. "For I am the LORD, your God, who takes hold of your right hand and says to you, Do not fear; I will help you" (Isaiah 41:13). The Lord wanted to begin healing those old abandonment issues I had been clinging to. He wanted me to understand that I could cling to Him as He held my right hand. He would not abandon me.

This was a powerful visual to me. I had no idea at the time that Christian counselors often ask their patients to go back to a difficult memory to try to picture Jesus with them. This helped me understand the importance of training our memories to include God. When we do this, we are able to see the Lord bringing His very presence to our experiences.

Not long afterward, another familiar verse ministered to me in a fresh way. My husband pointed out something that I had not noticed before. "The LORD is close to the brokenhearted and saves those who are crushed in spirit" (Psalm 34:18).

"Marilyn," Paul asked, "where does the Lord say He is in relationship to the brokenhearted?"

I looked again at the verse. "He says He is *close* to the brokenhearted. Oh, wow, He's right next to me!" I said with a new understanding. The Lord then showed me a verse that has remained a visual for me: "He [God] stands at the right hand of the needy one" (Psalm 109:31). I smiled as I looked to my right and said, "Father, I know You are standing right next to me and You're holding my right hand. Thank You!"

Two years later the Lord would take me to a deeper place in another memory, my secret memory, but first He wanted to continue to teach me more on the subject of forgiveness. He had a whole lot more to teach me about shame as well.

I finally admitted that people can and do hurt other people. They can abandon you, deceive you, betray you, abuse you, and drop you off alongside the road. As much as we'd like, we do not have trial-free lives. I'm thankful that Scripture says, "Here on earth you will have many trials and sorrows" (John 16:33, NLT), because that tells me I'm normal. Jesus told His close disciples, "You are those who have stood by me in my trials" (Luke

22:28). Even Jesus had trials. Jesus was abandoned, deceived, betrayed, and abused. Jesus was forced to walk down the road with His cross while the crowds jeered. Jesus didn't escape trials and sorrows in this world—and He was perfect! Doesn't it only make sense that we will experience trials and sorrows as well? How thankful I am that the Lord Jesus understands the trials we go through, whether they are brought on by our choices, other people, or circumstances. We have a High Priest who is able to sympathize with our weaknesses (see Hebrews 4:14).

Jesus knows when another person demolishes us, and it must deeply grieve Him. He totally understands because it happened to Him. "He was despised and rejected—a man of sorrows, acquainted with deepest grief" (Isaiah 53:3, NLT).

Once during my quiet time I took a good look at Matthew 27. I read about the wounds that were inflicted on Jesus. He truly was acquainted with grief—and grief from *me*. I listed some of the ways Jesus suffered during His last hours on earth. I have kept this list and refer to it often:

For me and you, Jesus was:

slapped
flogged
stripped
mocked
cut by a crown of thorns
struck on the head—again and again
insulted
mocked
beaten
sneered at
pierced
crucified

And in the previous chapter of Matthew, we read that, right before all of the above happened: "All the disciples deserted him and fled" (26:56). The Old Testament book of Isaiah gives us, through a prophetic view, a picture of what Jesus went through. "I offered my back to those who beat me, my cheeks to those who pulled out my beard; I did not hide my face from mocking and spitting" (Isaiah 50:6). The King James Version reads, "I hid not my face from shame and spitting." It was interesting to me how shame and spitting were put together.

In Psalm 69:19-21, David wrote what the future Messiah would experience: "You know how I am scorned, disgraced and shamed; all my enemies are before you. Scorn has broken my heart and has left me helpless; I looked for sympathy, but there was none, for comforters, but I found none. They put gall in my food and gave me vinegar for my thirst." The Lord experienced physical, emotional, religious, and verbal abuse. He definitely knows what it's like to hurt physically, mentally, spiritually, and emotionally.

When I first looked at that list I really didn't give much thought to being sneered at or spat upon. (Then I remembered how much I dislike getting dirty looks from other drivers.) I can't imagine the kind of sneers Jesus received. Nor can I imagine being spat upon. Have you been sneered at or deliberately spat upon? As far as I'm concerned, sneering and spitting at a person are two powerful tools of shaming.

In addition to His physical pain, Jesus also felt the pain of our sin. Sin pain. "He . . . who knew no sin" (2 Corinthians 5:21, NKJV) took on our sin. That means Someone who never sinned or felt the agony of committing a sin was now feeling all of our combined sins! Think about how you'd feel if someone slandered you. You would feel that pain. Now multiply that pain with every sin out there and imagine feeling that! It is a pain I cannot and will never be able to conceive.

Name any sin:

  gossip
  stealing
  deceit
  lying
  addictions
  affairs
  pornography
  rape
  murder
  fill in the blank _____

Whatever sin you can think of, Jesus felt it in His body as He was on the cross. He truly felt *your* pain. It was as if God took all of our sins, compressed them into a weight, and then laid it on Jesus. Heavy, heavy stuff.

Recently I pictured in my mind Jesus struggling up the hill of Calvary carrying a huge burden on His back. Then it hit me: *my* sin was in that burden on His back too! I wasn't only someone who had been *offended* by a difficult person; I had also been an *offender*. I found what theologian Karl Barth said to be true for me: "Even if the debts of our offenders appear to us to be very heavy, they are always infinitely lighter than ours with God."[1]

Yet Jesus, weighed down with the pain of every sin imaginable (mine included), says right in the middle of this excruciating time, "Father, forgive them."

He did not wait until He was resurrected or until He got to heaven (when He'd feel good again) to ask His Father to forgive us. He didn't wait for us to say we were sorry before forgiving us either. No! He asked His Father to forgive us in the *middle* of His pain—the pain *we* were causing Him.

I received many letters from people after my story first aired on the *Focus on the Family* radio program. Sadly, many people wrote words like this: "Marilyn, if you only knew what this difficult person did to me. There is no way on earth I can forgive him. I'll forgive him when I get to heaven."

I feel sad when I read letters like that. Oh sure, most of those who wrote suffered ghastly abuse. My story pales significantly in comparison to many of their experiences. I wish I had kept track of how many people wrote, "Your dad was just like mine, except mine was also an alcoholic." Or "my dad sexually abused me." Or "my mother hated me and favored my sibling." Yet here is a conclusion I have come to. When I get to heaven, forgiveness will be unnecessary since we'll all be perfect. The place I can give forgiveness is here on earth.

Just think, even as mankind was *rejecting* Christ by allowing Him to die on the cross, He was *accepting* us. Even today, He is ready to help anyone and is not shocked by anything: "Jesus the Son of God . . . understands our weaknesses, for he faced all of the same testings we do, yet he did not sin. So let us come boldly to the throne of our gracious God. There we will receive his mercy, and we will find grace to help us when we need it most" (Hebrews 4:14–16, NLT). There is no way I can comprehend that kind of acceptance. What unexplainable, amazing grace! That is extreme forgiveness.

How grateful I am that God can forgive us both instantly and completely. I've often wished I could completely and totally forgive someone at the snap of a finger. Thankfully, the Lord understands that it's generally difficult for us to forgive immediately. Often forgiveness is a process that must be worked through.

Not many months ago, I was at a conference center getting ready to speak for a women's retreat when a young woman came up to me and asked me to pray for her. She told me that her sister had not talked to her in years. They had called a family meeting, had an intervention, and even had their pastor go over to their home to try to help mediate between the family members. Their church family had faithfully prayed for years for them, but nothing worked. Now this young woman told me her sister was also at this retreat. She mentioned that it was awkward, but she asked if I would pray that the Lord would restore their relationship. She was open to it, but her sister remained closed and resistant.

At the end of the retreat we had a closing service where women could share what they sensed God had put on their hearts during the weekend. All of a sudden a woman got up and went to the microphone and began crying. She announced to everyone that she had been wrong to give her sister the silent treatment for so many years. Then, in front of everyone, she looked at her sister who was sitting in the audience and asked her to forgive her. These were the sisters who had been at odds with each other.

I sat in the back of the conference room as I watched the other sister get out of her chair, run down the aisle, and engulf her sister in a hug. They stood saying to each other there in front of all of us, "I'm so sorry . . . please forgive me." The whole audience was crying and applauding. They knew the two sisters' history and had prayed for resolution for years. The audience and I watched in amazement as the two sisters reconciled. We actually watched forgiveness happen!

Can you imagine how the Father responds when He sees His children forgiving one another? I'm sure He's cheering, weeping, and clapping just as we did at that closing session of the retreat.

Our relationships and the way we treat each other are

important to our heavenly Father. When our children were young and one of them was mean to a sister or brother, it hurt *me*. I also remember how wonderful I felt when the children made up with each other. I believe God feels that same way.

By the way, sometimes granting forgiveness too quickly can be damaging because we haven't yet taken the time to acknowledge and work through our hurt. There are times when a person may suddenly ask you to forgive them for an extremely difficult transgression. (I'm thinking here of someone who may have abused you in some way.) You know it's right to forgive them, but you haven't had time to process it. You may even feel if you forgive them right then and there they are getting off too easy. But because you know you should forgive, you say, "Okay, I forgive you." Inside, however, you really weren't prepared to offer forgiveness and needed more time. When my daughter Amanda and I were talking about the danger of forgiving too quickly, she compared it to a doctor who stitches up a wound before the infection had been fully cleaned out. It looks fine for a little bit, but eventually the infection grows even more fierce because it hasn't been addressed and has nowhere to go. It just festers under the skin until it eventually spreads to other parts of the body.

A few years ago the Lord used a visual concept by author and counselor Dr. Chuck Lynch to help me when I knew I needed to forgive someone but just couldn't forgive that person immediately. After all, some sins against us are so horrendous that forgiving instantaneously is very difficult. Chuck suggests that when a person has hurt us, we put him or her in what he calls the "Jesus Jail."[2] Picture a jail. Then visually place the person who is hurting you or has hurt you into that jail. You don't leave the person there permanently, only while you are in the process of forgiving that individual. By putting someone in the Jesus Jail, you are saying to the Lord, "I relinquish my desire to take out revenge on this person. I will not return evil for evil. I am placing this person in Your hands so *You* may deal with them in Your own time and way."

The Jesus Jail helps us release the person to Christ and allows Him to work with him or her—and us. If we allow Him, God patiently helps us move toward forgiveness. The Holy Spirit gently whispers to us, "Forgive that person who hurt you, My child, for it is the only way to take something bad and turn it around for good."

Someone hurt a family member of ours a few months ago. My mother's heart went out to this family member, and I felt frustrated at the person who had done the damage. Immediately I knew I was supposed to forgive the offender, but my emotions were too raw at that moment. I remember visually placing that person in the "Jesus Jail" and saying to the Lord, *I give them to You; please help me get to the place of truly forgiving them.* Every so often I would start stressing out about that person and situation. Then I would have to take a deep breath and remember that I had placed them in the Jesus Jail under the watchful eye of the true Judge. (Sometimes I had to do this several times a day.) He was handling them, and by taking my hands off, it allowed the Holy Spirit to work as He desired. Three months later the Lord allowed me to fully forgive that person. I was ready, and the forgiveness I felt toward that person was sincere. I opened the door of the Jesus Jail and freed this individual. Actually, I really freed myself.

God's Word tells us to "bear with each other and forgive whatever grievances you may have against one another. Forgive as the Lord forgave you" (Colossians 3:13). I am so grateful that whenever I ask the Lord to forgive me, He does. Why, then, is it so hard for me to extend forgiveness to *others*? As I read that verse I see I have no option other than to forgive. The verse doesn't say *try* to forgive. It simply says *forgive*.

What does it mean to "bear with" one another? I had an interesting discussion about this verse with my son-in-law, John, a doctoral candidate at Princeton Theological Seminary. He told me, "'To bear' in this verse means to have compassion on a person, even when his or her actions and attitudes are wrong. We are to bear with a person who is annoying, troublesome, needy, even disobedient—just as God bears with us." But John also added, "To bear with someone does *not* mean we make excuses for them. We don't ignore or blow off people's wrongdoings. The Lord didn't make excuses for us. He judged us as sinners while taking that judgment upon Himself."

My son-in-law concluded, "To forgive 'as the Lord forgave us' is not just a word or feeling, it is a practice—*a way of treating people*. Bearing with a person gives them the opportunity to deal with the consequences of their sin, to have some space and time to be convicted by the Holy Spirit, to repent, and hopefully to grow."

I admit, though, sometimes I think that if I forgive difficult people, they will be free and off the hook. They can go on in life as if nothing happened, which seems unfair to me. I've learned, however, that when I let people off the hook through forgiveness, the Lord will continue to work with them because they are still on God's hook. He is not finished with them yet. Once we leave them with God, He can deal with them in the ways He knows are best. Over and over again Scripture makes this clear. "Do not say, 'I'll pay you back for this wrong!' Wait for the LORD, and he will deliver you" (Proverbs 20:22). Revenge is unnecessary because Scripture promises, "God is just: He will pay back trouble to those who trouble you and give relief to you who are troubled" (2 Thessalonians 1:6-7). Releasing an offender to God and taking our hands off the situation is a wise move. In fact, the Greek meaning of *forgive* is to "release" or "send off."

Author and speaker Jennifer Kennedy Dean shares the following story about her son which, for me, gives a wonderful illustration of the word *release.*

> When my son Stinson was a toddler, I picked him up from a birthday party he had attended. He came out proudly clutching a red, helium-filled balloon. "Stinson, what a wonderful balloon!" I said. "Don't let go of it or it will go way up in the sky and we won't be able to get it back."
>
> I turned around for a moment, and when I turned back, there was Stinson, watching his wonderful red, helium-filled balloon float higher and higher. "Oh, I'm sorry you lost your balloon, Stinson," I said.
>
> "I didn't lose it, Mommy!" was Stinson's reply. "I gave it to Jesus!"[3]

"I gave it to Jesus." Release! It is so hard to do with difficult people or difficult situations, but so freeing!

I've realized something else about forgiveness. Sometimes we will have to do what I call "reforgive." I don't mean to sound contradictory, but I know how our human nature can act sometimes. We believe we have truly forgiven someone and then out of the blue we are hit with the thought, *But he did such and such to me!* Perhaps your wedding invitations had just been mailed when your fiancé unexpectedly called off the wedding. Through time and forgiveness you go on. But then you see the nonreturnable wedding dress you purchased hanging in the closet. Ouch! Reforgive. Or perhaps your spouse had an affair; you've worked through all those dynamics; you're finally doing well; and then it hits you again . . . *my spouse betrayed me!* Reforgive.

I wonder if this reforgive thing is similar to that red "restart" button on my electrical switch plate. Sometimes when the power circuit shuts down we have to push the restart button. It's okay to do that; that's what it's there for. At such times, you might pray: *Father, You know I've already forgiven that person, but today I am having a hard memory or bad thoughts about her. Please enable me to have fresh grace to give another push to the forgiveness restart button. I reforgive her right now with Your help.*

In a sense, that's what I had to do that day when the memory of being left on the road cropped up. I think sometimes God allows the memory of a very specific injury to resurface because it needs to be dealt with individually. Before that, I knew I had forgiven my dad with a broad stroke of forgiveness. The Lord reopened this wound, however, so I could reforgive. In this instance, I needed to deal with the intense anger I felt over my dad's actions. I had pushed my anger down because I thought it was sinful to feel that way. How thankful I am that the Lord revealed my anger so I could release it.

In addition, remembering that incident allowed me to see that Jesus was there with me. When the pain from a difficult past experience begins to build, I've learned to look at that situation and say, "Father, even though I don't understand why this happened, I know without a doubt that You were there with me." Next, I look for the ways God showed up. As a result, my memory of being left on the side of the road is now a memory of Jesus and me—*together*—forever etched in my mind.

I also realized something else through that time of reforgiving. The Lord helped my love for my dad to deepen. He enabled me to have a genuine love and acceptance of my father in spite of his shortcomings. I also began to get a glimpse of how a perfect God can use an imperfect parent (something I especially appreciate now as I parent). While my dad would not have qualified for the Father of the Year Award and he made some extremely unwise parenting choices, I can be grateful that my dad gave me life. Second, God used him to help shape my character and who I am today. In addition to that, my dad, without realizing it, helped me see my neediness for God and nudged me toward dependency on my heavenly Father. I am grateful to have had the dad I did for those reasons.

I can look back at him now and laugh about some things he did. I can laugh about the way he played both an invisible trombone and Jew's harp. I can laugh as I remember how he constantly lost his car keys and asked my mother where they were even though she never drove. I can laugh as I remember the time when he worked the third shift in our post office and heard strange noises. Thinking there were robbers in the building, he frantically called the police. It turns out the robbers were just a box of parakeets that was ready to be shipped out. My dad ended up being featured in our local paper the next day. I'm grateful for the laughter—it's healing.

My earthly father is in heaven now, and I look forward to seeing him one day. (By the way, my dad is no longer imperfect.) I long to put my arms around him and say, "Daddy, I love you, and I look forward to spending eternity with you." I know he won't push me away when I hug him. He and I will both be redeemed shame lifters.

A couple of years after the healing of that memory of being left on the road, the Lord wanted to reopen another wound— the one secret I had concealed and thought I'd locked away permanently. That was about to change.

HOW ABOUT YOU?

1. I believe that sometimes when we are wounded, especially as children, we do not know how to grieve the wound or have it "dressed" properly. We just go on with life. The Lord sometimes allows these memories to come to light to remove built-up scar tissue and to give us a time to grieve and heal properly. Can you recall a time when a painful memory resurfaced? Did it allow you to experience a deeper emotional healing?

2. Dr. Robert Enright says, "a grudge is an anger that won't quit."[4] Are you avoiding anyone because he or she "bugs" you or are you holding a grudge against that person? What first step might you take to restore this relationship? By the way, it takes two to reconcile, but it only takes one to extend forgiveness. (Note: There are some people we need to avoid because they are not "safe people" for us to be around. We can forgive them, but reconciliation might not be advisable.)

3. Author John Stott says, "Before we can begin to see the cross as something done for us, we have to see it as something done by us."[5] Spend some time reading Matthew 27, which recounts Christ's death on the cross. Write down all of the injuries that were done to Him. Keep this list handy.

4. What sin committed against you has been the hardest for you to forgive?

5. Do you feel burdened by a sin you committed that you're sure God would not want to forgive? If so, explain.

   The apostle John reminds us, "If we confess our sins to him, he can be depended on to forgive us and to cleanse us from *every* wrong" (1 John 1:9, TLB, italics mine). Psalm 103:12 also mentions that God removes our sin as far as the east is from the west. We know where the north and south poles are, but where do east and west meet? We can't go there. God removes our sin and it's gone!

6. Do you need to temporarily place someone in the "Jesus Jail" (see pages 118–119) while you work with the Lord on the issue?

7. "Make allowance for each other's faults, and forgive anyone who offends you. Remember, the Lord forgave you, so you must forgive others" (Colossians 3:13, NLT). What comes to your mind as you read those words?

8. Can you think of some offense you've recently had to "release" or "send off" that would illustrate the meaning of forgiveness? Explain.

9. Is there anyone you need to reforgive because his or her name and the offense keep coming to your thoughts?

※　　※　　SHAME $\mathcal{L}$ifters　　※　　※

- Have you stopped speaking to a friend or family member because of a disagreement? Take the initiative, along with a humble spirit, and seek to break the silence. You may be rejected, but at least you will have pursued peace. (Note: Unless you have a counselor helping you, I don't recommend trying to initiate a conversation like this with an "unsafe" person—for instance, someone who is abusive.)
- Would you like the most *refreshing* experience possible? Would you believe it's to *repent*? Acts 3:19 says, "Repent, then, and turn to God, so that your sins may be wiped out, that *times of refreshing may come from the Lord*" (italics mine). Sit down and ask God if there is anything you need to repent from. If something comes to mind, write it down. Next write Acts 3:19 across it and then rip it up and throw it away. It's gone!
- When you're ready to forgive a person who has hurt you,

purchase a helium-filled balloon. Let that balloon represent the offense. Next, ask God to help you "release" (or "send off") that person's offense by cutting the string and allowing the balloon to float up to your ceiling. Allowing it to stop at the ceiling is a visual reminder that Satan will seek to stop you from forgiving. He will try to put a limit or a "ceiling" on how far you go with forgiveness. In your mind's eye, see your balloon going all the way to Jesus. It is so freeing!

Dear heavenly Father,
Thank You that You are the one and only perfect Father. Both Your love and understanding of me are unlimited (Psalm 147:5).

Thank You that Jesus died for my sins. Thank You that when I confess my sins You have provided a way for me to be forgiven of any sin I may have committed—removed as far as the east is from the west—gone! (Psalm 103:12). My repentance, combined with Your forgiveness, brings wonderful times of refreshment to my soul (Acts 3:19-20).

Help me to remember that just as You forgive me, You also forgive those who sin against me. Sometimes I act as if forgiveness only extends one way. And please help me get to the place where I can "release" or "send off" to You the person who has hurt me. Thank You that You are never reluctant to extend forgiveness to all who ask (Acts 10:43). And thank You that You do not hold grudges (Psalm 103:8-9). In Your cleansing and freeing name, Amen.

NINE

Intermingling the Good and the Bad

Where there is ruin, there is hope of treasure.
—Rumi, thirteenth-century Persian poet

The door I had kept so tightly locked and secured to safeguard my secret was finally cracked open without even a squeak. It happened that day when a woman told me I had a "shame-based perspective of life."

I didn't like what I saw behind the door as I hesitantly allowed myself to quickly glance inside. I saw a person who was difficult to get along with—myself. Deep down, one side of me knew I was a fairly healthy and well-adjusted person, yet another part of me couldn't fully accept myself. I felt a constant pull back and forth between these two views. I lived in the middle of that tension. People would probably have said I was easygoing enough, but inside I was at war against myself. A walking civil war. I was my own difficult person!

It was at that point I fled to my bedroom closet and, face-down in white rug fuzz, poured out my thoughts to the Lord. After that I purposely got quiet. The Lord then took me on a "controlled" guided tour back into my memories . . . very slowly and carefully.

He gently pushed the door open a bit wider. I gasped. I had been in the dark so long about my shame that when I started

129

to see myself it looked as if everything was wrecked. For the first time I truly allowed myself to think about that devastating secret incident from my early childhood. It was as if a powerful lamp penetrated down into deep waters. I had not gone there before. I always knew the memory was lying in the depths of my mind, but I had refused to look at it. The memory was a shipwreck lying silently, ghostlike on the black floor of the ocean. I allowed myself to peer even deeper into the darkness. And as my eyes adjusted to that darkness, scenes took shape and came to light.

I watched as a teen who was staying in a house led a little girl to her bedroom. He took off her clothes. Her face immediately darkened in fear. She knew something wasn't right. He pushed her down on the floor between the bed and wall and held down her arms. He did things to her that should have never happened to her or anybody else. She cried and cried and asked him to stop. She struggled to get up but he held her down even though she begged to be released. When he was finished, he told her not to tell anyone, especially her parents. If she did she would be in "big trouble." Her face expressed fear. It also reflected a sad, submissive look. She was convinced that her parents would punish her for such an awful act. She would keep the little secret so her parents would not be angry with her.

So the guest came to her again—another day. This time she felt fear mixed with hate. She again cried for help. This time someone else was in the room. Their eyes met. She pleaded for help. The person turned away and did not intervene.

I ran from that open door of my heart, sobbing. I knew who that little girl was. It was me! I was in ruins. What was I supposed to do with what I saw? They were memories. *My* memories—memories that had been there all the time but memories I had purposely refused to deal with.

When one feels shame and then has to openly face shameful experiences on top of that internalized shame, it produces even *more* shame. That's why I had kept quiet and didn't want to talk about my abuse. That's why I had felt trapped by shame and fear. Anytime you talk about your shameful experiences, you feel that same shame all over again.

But something good happened the day that door to my secret was opened. For the first time, I acknowledged to myself—and then to my husband—that I had been sexually abused. (Before our marriage, I had told Paul only that I'd been sexually "mistreated" as a child. At my request, he did not bring it up again. But things were changing. I was now free to tell him.) Dr. Dan B. Allender defines sexual abuse as involving "any *contact* or *interaction* whereby a vulnerable person (usually a child or adolescent) is used for the sexual stimulation of an older, stronger, or more influential person."[1]

Now I knew that the woman's words spoken to me were true. I *did* have a shame-based perspective of life, but I had never realized it before. The shame inflicted when I was abused silently grew and affected my whole being. That's what shame does—it grows in secret, dark places until exposed to light and truth.

I again went facedown in the rug and cried out to God for a very long time. Finally, when there seemed to be no more tears, I lay there. In that quietness I heard a soft, still, small voice whisper to my heart.

Marilyn, describe in one word how you felt when you relived those memories. I knew it was the gentle voice of my heavenly Father. It was so real, so peaceful.

I had to think for only a few seconds. *Father, I felt powerless! I couldn't get up, he held down my arms, he wouldn't go away, and he made me promise I wouldn't tell anyone. I couldn't do anything. I was powerless!*

Marilyn, I, too, was powerless at one time, came a soft reply.
*I understand. My arms were also held down by people while they did
cruel things to Me. I, too, was stripped of My clothing and then nailed
on a cross with My arms stretched open. I could not get up. I was powerless against them.*

I hadn't thought about Jesus' death like that before—that
He felt powerless. I pictured His arms being held down and
stretched open as if trying to embrace the entire world. *Lord, I
still feel like I was forsaken and left alone.*

*My child, I, too, felt alone as I groaned aloud My deepest question,
"'Father, why have You forsaken Me?'" Yet even though I was rendered
powerless, did you realize that My last words on the cross were not,
"'Father, why have You forsaken Me?'"*

No, I hadn't thought of that before, I admitted. *But, Lord, one of
the times I was held down someone else was standing in the room. That
person ignored my pleading for help and turned away. I was forsaken by
that person.*

*I understand, My child. There were people all around Me, and no
one helped Me either.*

I tried to absorb the scene of Jesus being held down on
a cross with many people around Him and no one coming
forward to help Him. He also felt that everyone, including His
Father, had forsaken Him. I tried to imagine all the hideous
verbal abuse hurled at Him, the thick spit running down His
body by those who had spat upon Him, and His horrendous
physical pain. Then this realization hit me—*my* sin had
molested Him. *My* sin had bruised and abused Him! *My* sin
had held Him down on the cross. And I wept even more. He
experienced powerlessness for me. I grabbed a pen and paper
and journaled the many thoughts that flooded into my soul
that day.

"Marilyn, My child, it's okay," I wrote as I heard the Lord

speak to my heart. "When I was crucified on the cross for your sins, I also crucified your embarrassment and shame. I completely scorned shame for you as I endured the cross. Do you know how I handled all of that shame? My last act on the cross was to commit Myself into My heavenly Father's hands. *Those* were my last words: 'Father, into Your hands I commit My spirit.' You must also commit your crushed spirit into My hands to be delivered from the effects of your shame.

"Remember, too, that I did not remain on the cross. I rose from the dead. I have resurrection power. You are no longer powerless either. My resurrection power is available to you as well. What is resurrection power? It is the same mighty power that raised Me, Jesus, from the dead and is the power at work within you. You actually have My Holy Spirit living in you—the power of the Spirit of God. Never forget that I am an all-powerful God. It is who I am and always will be. People can oftentimes misuse power, but it is against My holy nature to abuse power. My power raises you up—up from the grave of abuse, up from the grave of sin, up from the grave of shame. There is no power on earth like My resurrection power."

Then I remembered a portion of a verse I had learned as a young adult: "I want to know Christ and *the power of his resurrection* and the fellowship of sharing in his sufferings, becoming like him in his death" (Philippians 3:10, italics mine). I began to experience and to acknowledge the power of His resurrection in my life for the very first time. He was lifting my life from the tomb of shame and giving me a new way of living. As I continued to listen quietly before the Lord, He began to heal my very old heart wound. The Lord gave me His power back! Not only did He help me recognize and refuse to carry my shame any longer, He made me realize that whenever I slip back into the old shame mode, I have God's power to pull me out.

How thankful I am for Dr. Dan Allender's words, "[Our] memories are being used by God to transform us, not destroy us."[2] I never dreamed that God would be able to use horrible memories to repair me. Only He can do that. Oh, I wish I had allowed myself to revisit my bad memories years before.

The most helpful thing I did soon after I acknowledged my shame was talk to someone else about it. My husband was one of those people. He was so understanding. I also talked with a counselor and attended a Christian conference on sexual abuse. The shackles of shame began to fall off. Having a trusted, empathetic, grace-filled person listen to you provides a healing balm.

I'll admit, though, that when I finally allowed myself to recall the abuse, I was angry with the person who had intruded into my life and abused me at a young age. How dare he do that! He probably had children of his own by now—how would he have felt if someone had abused them? I hadn't dealt with the buried anger before because I would not allow myself to face the fact that I had been abused.

In addition to the rise of anger, I felt some strange comfort in viewing myself as a victim. It gave me "rights"—rights to stay angry, rights to hold a grudge (which is low-grade anger), and rights to hope the Lord got even with my abuser. I believe I needed to see myself as a victim, at least for a while. For too long I had thought that somehow I was responsible for the abuse that happened to me. It was healing for me to understand that I was an innocent victim.

The Lord, however, didn't want me to remain in this victim mode. Nor did He want me to see myself merely as a survivor. Instead He wanted me to go on to become a victor because of His healing. He began to show me the meaning behind "resurrection power." I would receive power in *laying down my life, my rights, and my power*—which sounded so paradoxical to me. However, that is exactly what Jesus did on the cross when He committed His spirit into the hands of His heavenly Father. First Peter 2:23 says of Jesus on the cross: "When they hurled their insults at him, he did not retaliate; when he suffered, he made no threats. Instead, he *entrusted himself to him who judges justly*" (italics mine).

By the way, I'm not suggesting that I became a doormat and accepted what my abuser did. No, the Lord began to show me that, while it was true the intruder had brought deep shame on me and I wasn't to blame, I didn't have to continue living in shame. I could talk about the incident and didn't have to keep it a secret. I could move on. Also, if I allowed it, I could entrust myself to the One who judges justly. (Let me be quick to say that an abuser needs to be brought to light and action taken. But if that doesn't happen, we still are responsible for our own actions and attitudes. We must choose to begin the journey toward healing.) Shame doesn't go away by hiding it or by punishing an abuser or ourselves. Shame only dissipates through forgiveness, love, and grace.

Right after the Lord brought my shame out in the open, He used Rokelle Lerner, a conference speaker, to provide a visual of what it means to put away shame. She suggests mentally picturing yourself filling a basket with all the shame your abuser inflicted on you. Next, picture your abuser. Then say to the one who violated you, "I do not have to carry this shame any longer; it all belongs to you." And finally, in your mind's eye, hand the basket of shame to your abuser. This exercise was instrumental in my being able to release the shame so that it was placed where it rightfully belonged. It made such a difference to know the abuse I experienced was not *my* fault.

How wonderful to realize that, thanks to His work on the cross, the Lord takes our basket of shame from us. It's as if Jesus took on Himself the whole world's basket of shame, then dumped it back on Satan and said, "Here, this all belongs to you. I scorned all shame."

Something else happened to me when I released my shame. Since my teen years I had had a troublesome, recurring dream. It was always the same: I could see myself standing in front of my bedroom closet in my childhood home. As I looked into the closet I saw mostly empty hangers. There were only a couple pieces of shabby clothing hanging there. I had a very hard time trying to find something to wear to school. Finally, I pulled out a piece of ragged clothing and tried to cover myself as best I could. I felt so ashamed of those clothes. When I got to school a group of friends encircled me as if to shield me. They did not laugh at me. In fact they were silent, but they surrounded me so no one would see my skimpily clad body. I knew my friends were embarrassed and felt sorry for me but just weren't telling me. The dream ended with me walking down the school hallway feeling humiliated and embarrassed. How I hated that dream!

The day I faced my abuse the disturbing dream stopped. In fact it was on that very day that the Lord revealed to me what was behind my dream: *shame.* For so many years I had tried to figure it out. That day all the pieces came together.

My bedroom closet represented my inner self. It revealed that I believed I was lacking and ragged—there was nothing worth pulling out to wear in public. *I* was convinced that I was not worth much. If only I could cover myself with "clothes" of perfectionism then others would not see my shabby inside. Friends tried to come alongside to help, but it was never enough. The shabby pieces of clothing that had hung in the closet of my dreams and in my real-life heart revealed how shame, like a moth, had silently eaten little holes into my very being.

I also realized from the dream that once shame becomes internalized, it permeates your subconsciousness and your dreams. Yet at the same time, it's strange how you can be so unaware of its presence—just as you can be unaware of shame when you are awake.

In addition, after a while you don't necessarily need painful circumstances or an abusive person to ignite your feelings of shame because they already burn within you. *You* become the one who stokes the embers of shame to keep it going, allowing it to carry out its deadly orders of devaluing yourself. Self destroys self. Not only can shame lead to outwardly destructive acts like addictions, depression, and rage, it can cause a person to be less spontaneous and more cautious in an attempt to avoid any additional threat to his or her survival.

This wake-up call from my dream showed me that I needed to exchange the shabby shame clothing for new clothes—a white robe of righteousness from my Savior. Jesus is the only One who could, with my permission, begin to remove my shame.

I love the story of King Jehoiachin in 2 Kings 24 and 25. In fact, I believe it is one of the most incredible stories of shame and grace in the Bible.

King Jehoiachin was eighteen years old when he was crowned king of Judah, but he "did evil in the eyes of the LORD" (24:9). His forefathers, in whose footsteps he followed, were responsible for filling the streets with innocent blood (24:4). He reigned only three months before he had to surrender to King Nebuchadnezzar. Not only did King Jehoiachin have to submit to Nebuchadnezzar, he had to watch his mother, his attendants, his nobles, and all his officials surrender as well. Jehoiachin had failed to protect his people as king. He was disgraced and deported to Babylon along with thousands of others.

Then thirty-seven years later, an extraordinary thing happened to Jehoiachin. A new king by the name of Evil-Merodach replaced King Nebuchadnezzar, and he did something that doesn't make sense. He released Jehoiachin from prison! This former Judaean king did not deserve grace; he had done horrible, evil things as a king. Yet grace was still bestowed.

Jehoiachin's chains were removed, and Evil-Merodach "spoke kindly to him" (25:28). Not only was he given a seat of honor and food allowance, we read that the Babylonian king "supplied Jehoiachin with new clothes to replace his prison garb" (25:29, NLT). I am told that the phrase "he spoke kindly to him" has the meaning in Hebrew of "he lifted up his face." Evil-Merodach extended grace to a wicked, exiled king. Jehoiachin had his face lifted up; he was no longer downcast, he was no longer a prisoner clad in ragged garments. When people looked at Jehoiachin after that his face was clear and open—radiant! What a beautiful picture of shame being replaced with grace.

We don't know why Evil-Merodach acted as he did, but his actions do portray what Jesus Christ wants to do for us. He releases us from our prison and speaks kindly to us—He lifts our faces so we can look up. He replaces our filthy rags with a white robe of righteousness. And God raises us up with Christ and seats us with Him in the heavenly realms (Ephesians 2:6). We are invited to the banqueting table of the King of kings for eternity. What astonishing grace!

Recognizing the grace that Christ extended to me brought me full circle with my abuser. I no longer feel like the victim, nor do I feel any hatred toward him for what he did. I was victimized. I hated what he did to me. But I no longer carry that hatred or victimization inside of myself. I have been set free. And now I wonder, *who molested him?* What abuse did he experience that made him abuse others? He, too, was probably a victim of abuse.

I don't know if I will ever run into him here on earth, but he is forgiven. In my mind and heart I have chosen to "give" good back to him. (Remember the word *forgiveness* has *give* right in the middle.) I no longer want him to have to pay for what he did. But it has taken time and a long journey to get to that place. Richard Richardson writes, "When we do not forgive, we let the person who sinned against us control our life."[3] I didn't want that person to control my life any longer. And if Jesus, the *innocent* One, can forgive me, shouldn't I, the *guilty* one, be able to forgive others?

Now at this point, you may be thinking, *But the one who abused me was a loved one. How can I ever forgive that person?* Please, please get some godly professional help. Seek the Lord. But also remember that Jesus suffered and died because of *His loved ones.* He understands. Oh, what a price Jesus Christ paid for you to experience forgiveness. And what freedom there is in forgiveness! I love how it enables you to see treasure in the ruins.

Now, let me say a word to those who have done the abusing. Over the past few years, I have talked to abusers as well as the abused, and I know that your shame is often as deep as your victims'. God is reaching out to you as well. Jesus offers you His nail-scarred hand to give incredibly rich forgiveness and His resurrection power. He longs to work with your memories, your guilt, your shame, your sin, and your self-disgust.

You'll need to make some decisions, however. What are you willing to do about what you did? Are you willing to take responsibility for your wrongdoing and sin? Have you been confronted on this matter but refused to acknowledge your sin? Proverbs 13:18 describes a person who refuses discipline: "He who ignores discipline comes to poverty and *shame*" (italics mine). I have talked to many people who have been abused but whose abusers refused to admit the abuse. Again, this is shame holding back truth. Why? Anything you hold inside and keep secret is almost always bound up in shame.

After admitting the abuse, do you genuinely feel sorrow for the pain you have inflicted? Are you willing to connect with an effective, godly counselor? Proverbs 13:18 can also give you hope. The entire verse reads: "He who ignores discipline comes to poverty and shame, but whoever heeds correction is honored."

Next, are you willing to say you will never abuse like that again and have someone hold you accountable to that promise? Are you able to genuinely ask your heavenly Father to forgive you? *He is the one you have ultimately sinned against.* Are you willing, if possible and with the help of a counselor, to let the one you abused know you realize that you hurt that person deeply and ask for forgiveness? (Again, let me reemphasize to first seek the advice of a counselor to find out how and if you should communicate to the one you have abused.) He or she may not accept your actions of repentance, but God will—if you are honest and have a broken and contrite (repentant) spirit. God's Word says that He will not *ignore* or *despise* a person with a broken spirit (see Psalm 51:17). That is encouraging.

If you take responsibility for your actions you will, of course, face consequences (some of which you have probably already experienced). Thankfully, however, God has a wonderful "shame exchange program" for you. He will exchange your ashes of shame for His crown of beauty. He will exchange your mourning for the oil of His gladness. He will exchange your spirit of despair for a garment of praise (see Isaiah 61:3). That is good news! God's rehab program is thorough, and His restoration can penetrate to the very core of your being. He is able to make you a brand-new person.

One of my friends, whom I'll call Alicia, was abused by her father during most of her growing-up years. Later when she confronted her dad he denied it. Family members did not believe her either. When she was older, she completely severed her relationship with her father. Her children grew up never even seeing their grandfather because he was not a safe person to be around.

Just recently Alicia received a message that her father was dying from cancer and had only a few weeks left to live. My friend decided to take a risk and visit her parents' house where her dad was receiving hospice care. They had not seen each other for more than eighteen years. She clung to the verse, "[God] stands at the right hand of the needy one" (Psalm 109:31) as she drove to her parents' house.

She told me later, "Little did I know that when I saw my dad I would claim that verse for him. When I saw him, I saw Jesus at *his* right hand! Not only mine. He was a broken man when I saw him; my heart broke for him. My father looked very, very feeble and weak. I spent the entire time holding his hand. Amazing! Where his touch hurt me so much in the past, *my* touch definitely was healing for *him*."

Before Alicia left her parents' home, she prayed with her mom and dad and then bent down to give her dad a hug. As she did, her father whispered, "Let's just forget everything from the past, okay?" But before Alicia could respond, her dad quickly interjected, "No, I need to ask you to forgive me!"

My friend said, "I never thought I would hear him say those words, and I also realized that the forgiveness was already his. . . .

I didn't need to hear the words, but it was sure nice! I told him I'd forgiven him years ago, and I felt him tremble." Alicia's dad took ownership for his abuse for the very first time. A few days later he died in true peace.

Unfortunately, this man wasted many years by not owning up to his abuse sooner—and it didn't have to be that way. If you have been an abuser, you don't have to wait until you have only a few hours left on earth to make things right.

Perhaps you are neither an abuser nor a victim but maybe you *unintentionally* hurt someone. The serious consequences birthed toxic shame in you. Perhaps you lost your self-control and were faced with an unplanned pregnancy.

Or perhaps you accidentally hit and killed a pedestrian when you were driving. Though it was an accident, you felt horrible remorse and pain. Thoughts of "if only" immediately surface. *If only I had left the house a few minutes sooner; if only the pedestrian had been more visible.* Feelings of shame gradually took root as you rehearsed the scenario over and over again in your thoughts. You can't seem to move past the incident.

A tragic example of where these feelings can lead is found in the story of Cheung Shu-hung, who headed up the Chinese toy company Lee Der Industrial Company. Business was going well until 2007, when the business was forced to recall nearly one million preschool toys decorated with paint containing excessive amounts of lead. The recall cost his company $30 million. He could not bear the heaviness of the shame he felt he'd brought on himself and his country. His solution was to commit suicide.

Whether you are an abuser, an abused victim, or someone who accidentally caused pain to someone else, there is hope and healing for you. You don't have to be stuck in a frozen emotional state. You don't have to take your life. Jesus gave His life to remove the shame so you could live. I wish Cheung Shu-hung could have heard that good news. I pray no matter what you are dealing with right now that you will know and believe the good news—Jesus is your Shame Bearer.

My daughter Amanda, who along with her husband is currently a doctoral candidate at Princeton Seminary, and I were recently discussing Romans 8:28: "And we know that in all things God works for the good of those who love him." Amanda shared an interesting insight. This verse in the Greek could be understood to say that God can take all things—good and bad—and *intermingle* them together to make good. As you know, if you multiply a negative number by a positive one, you come up with a negative figure. However, in God's math, He multiplies the negative *and* positive and makes them, somehow, equal a positive. (Negative x Positive = Positive.) Only God can do that!

Intermingling the good and the bad was illustrated for me this past weekend. My husband, Paul, helped me husk dozens of ears of corn to get them ready to put in our freezer. I was just going out to the garbage can with the husks when Paul reminded me of our compost pile. He took the husks and silks from me and threw them on top of the pile in the backyard.

It is interesting how over time that garbage changes to rich, useful soil. Only God can do that! I almost missed having good soil by throwing away what seemed like useless garbage. We either take the junk in our life and stuff it in a garbage can that's taken out to a landfill and buried, or we allow God to throw it on His compost pile to produce a rich, transformed life.

Christ's body perhaps best illustrates how He takes the good and bad and intermingles them together. Look at the hands of Jesus, His brow, His feet, and His side. Those hideous, death-producing scars are ugly and revolting. Yet it is by those same horrible scars that we are healed. He intermingled His pure, holy self with our stinking sin so we could be righteous. Those hideous scars have become precious to us. One day we will see those very scars on the body of our Lord Jesus, and we will fall at His feet and worship the Lamb of God who was slain for us.

I wish bad things didn't have to happen to people, but after sin entered the world, pain and suffering became inevitable. Thankfully, God has a way of combining His grace, comfort, and hope with our difficult circumstances. In the process, He somehow brings good. As I handed my negative memory of abuse to the Lord that day in my closet, He took it and intermingled it with His resurrection power, showing me that I was no longer powerless. Jessie Penn-Lewis, the early twentieth-century British founder and editor of *The Overcomer* magazine, once observed: "The highest purpose of God in the believer is not to make him so much a powerfully-used instrument, as to bring forth in him the fullest manifestation of Christ in every aspect of His character, and this can only be done in the winepress valley of fellowship with His suffering."[4]

I needed Christ's resurrection power. Was I also, however, willing to say with the apostle Paul that "I want to know Christ and the power of his resurrection *and* the fellowship of sharing in his sufferings" (Philippians 3:10, italics mine)? Sure, I wanted to know Christ and to experience the power of His resurrection—but suffering? I appreciate Simone Weil's insight that "the extreme greatness of Christianity lies in the fact that it does not seek a supernatural remedy for suffering but a supernatural use for it."[5] Life on earth is full of hardships and suffering, but God has the ability to intermingle the very worst negative and the positive and use it for our good—a supernatural good.

God never wastes anything—including suffering. He is a

redeeming God. With that in mind, while I don't totally understand it, my sorrows and hardships are not wasted.

Two of the biggest questions I wrestled with as I thought
back on my abuse were, *Jesus, where were You?* and *Why didn't
You intervene?* Two answers have come to my heart and have
helped bring peace, even though these questions cannot be
fully explained. First of all, Jesus *was* with me. I have no question about that. He has revealed that over and over through His
Word, and His Word is truth. He was and is with you as well.
Second, Jesus *did* do something; He *did* intervene. He died on
the cross. He entered this sinful world where people have and
will continue to do horrendous things and He did something
about that evil. We may not see the good this side of heaven, but
we will one day. That's God's promise to us.

By the way, while it's easy for me to notice when others have
done wrong and have been "boundary breakers," I've realized
that we all are boundary breakers in some way. Every one of us
has sinned. How thankful I am that Jesus intervened and has tri-
umphed with good over evil.

Now I was armed with resurrection power and assumed I was
at the end of my journey of shame. I was moving forward until
my friend Lynn pointed out that I talked with an accent. Talked
with an accent? What in the world did she mean?

HOW ABOUT YOU?

1. The first step to releasing shame is to allow the Lord to help you
   open the door of your heart and face any bad memories that are
   shrouded in darkness. As Rick Richardson writes, "If God can heal
   our images, he can heal our heart."[6] What bad memories have
   you locked away?

2. Is your life open and transparent, or do you continue to hide any secrets? Why is it destructive to hold on to dark secrets of *any* kind?

3. According to Dr. Dan B. Allender's definition of abuse (see page 131), have you ever been sexually abused? (Note: I realize that this is an intensely personal question. Please give it some thought even if you do not write anything down. If you have been sexually abused and have not acknowledged it, please don't hold on to that secret as I did. Confide in a person whom you know to be safe. Please find a godly counselor in your area that comes highly recommended. Don't put it off. Just as if you found a tumor, you would make an appointment with a doctor for a diagnosis, so it is important to deal with the malignant tumor of shame.)

4. If you have abused someone (or know that you are currently abusing someone), what first step do you need to take to put an end to the abuse and resolve the hurt you have caused or are causing? (Note: Again, I know this is a very personal question. If you have been abusive, I would urge you to seek professional help if you haven't already done so.)

5. Describe any situation in which you felt powerless. What hope do we receive in 2 Corinthians 12:9 (NLT): "My grace is all you need.

My power works best in weakness"? Isaiah 40:28-31 reminds us of the powerful God we have and what He does for us: "He gives strength to the weary and increases the power of the weak" (v. 29).

6. Jesus' last words were "Father, into your hands I commit my spirit" (Luke 23:46). In what way do those words comfort us when we're hurting?

7. Psalm 31:5 also records these words: "Into your hands I commit my spirit. . . ." Take a moment to look up this passage. What additional information do we learn about God from the rest of that verse?

8. What does "resurrection power" signify to you (see page 133)?

9. What spoke to you the most in the story of Jehoiachin, king of Judah (2 Kings 24:8-16; 25:27-30)?

10. "We know that God causes everything to work together for the good of those who love God and are called according to his purpose for them" (Romans 8:28, NLT). Can you share an experience where God took your bad situation and intermingled it with His good? Or can you tell about a time when you found "treasure amidst the ruins"?

※　※　SHAME *Lifters*　※　※

- Many people attempt to skip over anger and jump immediately to peace. Doing so leads to a false peace. Anger is an emotion and an important stage in the grief process. Write down your anger. Cry out to God. Hit a pillow if you need to. Anger over injustice is righteous anger. You cannot release your anger until you acknowledge it.

- Write about a difficult situation you're dealing with now. Scripture tells us we *will* have trials and difficult times—it's normal. I've noticed, however, that it doesn't always explain *why* we have to go through them. Scripture also speaks about suffering (another normal part of our earthly lives) and how it can be used to bring glory to God. But again, we are not always told specifically *how* God does that. So even if your difficult situation makes no sense to you right now, try to compose a prayer or write a journal entry about it. Ask God to somehow intermingle his good with your bad situation and to enable it to bring glory to Him.

- If you've been abused, you may have accepted the blame for something that isn't your fault. If so, you might imagine yourself placing the shame you feel from that abuse in an imaginary basket. Then picture handing it back to your abuser. Or if anyone has shamed you in any other way, you can also imagine handing back that shameful experience to the person who caused it.

Dear heavenly Father,

Thank You for walking into the dark places of my life with me. As You do this, Your radiant light exposes and reveals areas that must be healed (John 12:46). You search out my woundedness whether I am aware of that woundedness or not.

You apply Your gentle pressure to the places that are bleeding, and I wonder if I can take any more. You use Your divine scalpel to cut out the old scar tissue, and I wonder if I can stand the pain (Psalm 147:3).

You then take my pain and intermingle it with Your power and You heal my memories, my attitudes, and my thoughts (Psalm 34:18). My pain is somehow transformed to be used for Your highest good and glory.

Thank You that You never abuse power (2 Peter 1:3). Thank You for being the God of resurrection (John 11:25). In Your all-powerful name, Amen.

TEN

Unlearning the Shame Language

> *To love myself is to accept God's evaluation instead of my own. And what a staggering value he places on each of us!*
>
> —Elizabeth Sherrill, *All the Way to Heaven*

Did I really speak with an accent? As I began to pay attention to my words, I realized my friend had correctly assessed my speech. When we live with shame for an extended period of time, we pick up an additional language. This "shame language" has a dialect all its own called lies. I did speak in two languages—English and shame with an accent in lies.

I was caught totally off guard by this discovery, however, because I had truly been working on releasing old shame patterns in my life. And I certainly didn't see myself as a liar. I thought I had been making progress. Shame is tricky, though, because it comes in layers. Finally, when I was able to peel off the layers of shame down to the core, I found the biggest surprise. In that core was a solid bedrock of lies!

Shame begins with lies, so it is only natural for the foundation of shame to be built on deceit. When something shameful happens to us, instead of getting past it, we generally beat ourselves up and think, *Why was I so dumb?* What a lie! Those lies pile up and get packed down hard by more layers of shame. I wonder if we have any idea of how these self-generated lies affect us. They continue to haunt our thoughts, and we in turn dwell on them and then finally feed off of them. We become what we think.

Another friend of mine noticed my "accent." I had been sitting in our church's café, the Gathering Grounds, with four other women. We were planning an evening of prayer for women to come together to pray specifically for the next generation. I was asked during that planning meeting if I would be willing to share some brief thoughts and lead the women in a time of intercessory prayer during the prayer service. I immediately cringed. I felt another woman in our group was much more qualified than I and I told the four women so. The group listened to me but tried to assure me I could do it. I insisted I couldn't. Finally someone else was assigned the job, and I accepted a less visible role.

When I got home later in the day, I saw I had an e-mail from one of the women at that planning meeting. This friend, Marlae, took a risk and in a truthful and grace-filled way shared her observations of me. She wrote: "Marilyn, one encouragement to you—I think it will help you to try and not verbally say negative things about yourself. You easily put yourself down verbally in front of others and no one else ever thinks that way about you. . . . I hope you will take this encouragement as it is meant from me—I feel bad when you put yourself down because you are such an awesome person who has so much to offer all of us. I love you."

Oops! My "inner dialogue disorder" was showing! How grateful I am that Marlae had the courage to speak truth into my life. I needed her to do that. She was actually being a shame lifter, a true giver of grace. I could receive her words of grace because I knew how much she loved me. Truth and love must always balance. It was definitely a wake-up call for me.

So often we are blind to our own weaknesses. I had not realized that I was putting myself down at that meeting. My friend's words—*and no one else ever thinks that way about you*—hit hard. Could that really be true? Since I believed people thought the same way about me as I did, I voiced negative statements about myself *before* they could. How wrong I was!

I also realized that when shame took over my life, my true identity was stolen. I was not the person the Lord had created me to be. For years I had believed the lies that I couldn't do things even though my true identity would quietly whisper in the background that I could.

Remember those credit-card identity theft commercials that show a person calmly speaking about all of their purchases? Like the little old lady who talks in a very manly voice about the monster truck she just bought? It's her body, but the wrong voice is coming out. Similarly, when I was battling shame, it was as if someone else took my identity and used it to make charges against me, leaving me to pay for those expenses. I believe that Satan seeks to steal your identity in Christ. It's your body, but he is saying things through you like, *I'm not good enough* or *I'm worthless.* It's the right body but the *wrong* voice.

Here are some examples of how spiritual identity theft happens. You are thinking you might like to teach a classroom of kids or present a workshop for adults. Then Satan whispers doubts, and the lies begin: *You better not teach people because they will find out you're really not so smart.* Or you consider trying out for the worship team or a music group. Satan defeats you by saying, *Better not use your talents publicly so no one ever hears your mistakes.* Or you dream about starting a new business or going on a missions trip. Satan once again comes to discourage you with words like, *I wouldn't dream about doing that—you'll probably fail.* Satan is known as the thief who "comes *only* to steal and kill and destroy" (John 10:10, italics mine).

Did you catch that word *only*? Satan has an agenda. He makes it his aim to steal the credit (value) we have in Jesus Christ by attacking our thoughts with self-doubt and lies. We believe deep down that God wants to use us, only to end up listening to the voice that tears us down. Sadly, we spend our lives listening, protecting, and nurturing these lies. It then becomes easy to speak these lies to ourselves and others. Shame truly is an identity crisis, and it loves to creep in and out of our lives.

When these lies were made known to me, I asked the Lord to help me understand and recognize His truth. I gave Him permission to teach me and to work the word *truth* into the fabric of my life. In fact, *truth* became my "Word for the Year" during that time. (Each fall I pray and ask the Lord to give me one word that He would like to work on in my life during the upcoming new year. By January I am ready with a new teaching word and look forward to what the Lord will show me over the course of the year. It's interesting that whatever the word is for the year, it comes up over and over again in my daily life and Bible reading. I also look for one or more Scripture verses that go with the word as well. I have used this process of a "Word for the Year" for over twenty-five years, and it has been an incredible teaching tool in my life.)

It was unbelievable how many times the word *truth* popped up in my everyday life as well as my Bible reading during the course of that year. Two of the key passages were: "For your love is ever before me, and I walk continually in your truth" (Psalm 26:3) and "I am the way and the *truth* and the life" (John 14:6, italics mine).

I had no problem with being truthful when I discovered that

my grocery store had failed to charge me for some flour tortillas. The next time I went to the store I gave them what I owed— that was easy. While I didn't want to lie to others, I had no trouble lying to one person . . . me! That revelation startled me. How could that be? Why did I find it okay to lie to myself while at the same time I sincerely did not ever want to lie to others? I believe it was because I was unaware of the subtleties of lying to myself. It had become second nature. Slowly, as if waking from a heavy sleep, I began to understand that God desired "truth from the inside out" (Psalm 51:6, *The Message*).

The lies the enemy tells each of us about ourselves can actually become *truth* to us. I really believed that I was not good enough to speak in front of people, that I didn't measure up to being a good wife, that I would become a burden to people, and that I was not confident or equipped to handle leadership positions. That to me was truth! Even though I knew the Lord had used me at times to speak to people, to be a helper to my husband, and to handle leadership positions, I *still* believed the lies. That is just another indicator revealing that shame exists. Shame, through lies, blinds you from seeing and enjoying the good you have done.

In the movie *The Princess Bride*, Princess Buttercup has a dream in which she is getting married. As she walks down the aisle at the start of the ceremony, an old, ugly woman gets up and starts booing her. As I began recognizing the lies I had accepted about myself, I realized I was just like Princess Butter-cup. I was walking down the aisle of life as the bride of Christ, fully accepted by Him, and at the same time I was hearing the overpowering boos from the enemy. Only this wasn't a dream in a movie, it was reality. The ugly old enemy of my soul had been seeking to distract, hinder, and destroy me. God, however, wanted to show me His truth and help me regain my true iden-tity: *His* princess bride.

I wondered if other people felt the same way I did. So I did a little survey. When I had an opportunity to speak to four hundred pastors' wives in another state, I asked them to write down one lie they believed about themselves. I didn't know if many would respond. I was overwhelmed as, one by one, women turned in their papers.

These were some of the common lies I read over and over:

I'm worthless.
I'm fat.
I'm stupid.
I'm not equipped to be a pastor's wife.
I'm not intelligent.
I'm not adequate as a mom.

Several wrote, "If people got to really know me, they wouldn't like me."

I was shocked! Maybe this was a problem *just* with pastors' wives. So I decided to ask another group of women, who were not pastors' wives and lived in another state, the same question.

The results, unfortunately, were pretty much the same. These were some of their responses:

I'm unworthy.
I'm fat.
I'm ugly.
I'm uneducated.
I'm slow.

And the one that really broke my heart was, "I don't want to look in the mirror anymore and see trash." Several other women simply wrote, "I am trash."

Those two unofficial surveys jolted me. Other people out there felt like I did. Since then I have done many more surveys, with the same results. Many people continually hear the booing coming from the enemy of their soul. What about you? Do you hear the booing? Do you believe any lies about yourself? You will not experience the life-transforming power of Jesus Christ by listening to your own shortcomings over and over. In fact, such lies set us up for shame.

Right after taking those two surveys, a young man involved in an international Christian ministry sent me an e-mail. He just happened to mention in his prayer newsletter that he was down and felt as if he were "a careless, irresponsible failure." Ouch!

Heavenly Father, what are You trying to tell me? I asked as I pondered those surveys. I guess most of us, men and women alike, believe lies about ourselves.

Around that same time one of my sons-in-law, Dave, another doctoral candidate at Princeton Seminary, was visiting. We were sitting at our kitchen table when he posed this question.

"Mom, who are you?"

I immediately responded, "I'm a wife, mother, pastor's wife, and . . ."

Dave stopped me from going further.

"No, Mom," he said gently, "those are your roles. I'm not asking what you *do*; I'm not asking about performance. I'm asking, *who* are you?"

His question made me think.

Tentatively I quietly said, "I'm God's child."

Dave smiled and nodded. "Go on," he urged.

"I'm God's beloved."

Dave added, "You're getting it. What else?"

With a bit more confidence I said, "I am a daughter of the King." And then it hit me. . . . "I am royalty!"

"Yes!" came Dave's confirming reply.

While I knew those things, why did the lies I believed about myself overshadow all the truth that God loves me as His child? One reason was my tendency to feel that I must *do something* in order for Jesus to love me. I needed to grasp that nothing I could do would make Him love me more. He already totally, unconditionally loves me more than I could ever fathom.

Scripture gives us a glimpse of the importance of who we are to God. "All things were created by him"—catch this next part—"and *for* him" (Colossians 1:16, italics mine). He not only made us, He made us *for Himself*. What great value He places on us! So what in the world was the root problem behind all of my thinking that I wasn't good enough? *Shame!*

Shame likes to cover God's truth with a wet, heavy blanket. It threatens to snuff out life. How was I going to throw back that wet, suffocating blanket? Only by believing and applying God's truth.

I turned to God's truth—His Word—to see what He had to say about His own Son. I knew God loved His Son, so I checked Scripture to see *why* God loved His Son. Surely, I thought, it was because of what Jesus *did* to earn that kind of love. I'm indebted to Rick Richardson and his insight of Luke 3:22. I knew this verse about Jesus, but I had missed something. As Jesus was being baptized "a voice came from heaven: 'You are my Son, whom I love; with you I am well pleased.'" God said He was well pleased with His Son, but for what reason? Jesus hadn't started His public ministry yet. He hadn't done any miracles. He hadn't even victoriously gone through the forty days of being tempted at that point. He was just *being* Jesus; He wasn't *doing*. In other words, God loved His Son not for His performance or His ministry, but God simply loved Him for who He was—His Son.

The Lord whispered to me, *Marilyn, when will you understand that I love you for who I made you to be, not for what you do? Do you remember holding your first granddaughter, Ella? You loved her! She had not done anything. You loved her because she was just being who she was supposed to be—a baby.*

The story of Jesus' baptism reminded me that God had repeated some of those same words to Jesus near the end of His ministry. After He had been transfigured before three of His disciples, God said, "This is my Son, whom I love; with him I am well pleased. Listen to him!" (Matthew 17:5). God was again affirming His Son. True, Jesus had done and accomplished much by then, but this time the Father added a command: "Listen to him!" After seeing Jesus transfigured in glorious, radiant light, the disciples wanted to *do* something. Peter suggested building three shelters: one for Jesus, one for Moses, and one for Elijah. God didn't want them to do something (perform), instead He wanted the disciples just to "Listen to him!"

Marilyn, the Lord added, *I want you to be still and listen to Me. If you listen to Me, you are going to know the truth, and the truth will set you free from the lies you believe about yourself.*

It wasn't long after my conversation with my son-in-law that I woke up in the middle of the night. I had been sleeping soundly when I heard a voice in my dream say rather loudly, "I am the way, the . . ." The voice stopped as if it was waiting for me to finish the sentence. Now fully awake, I sat up in bed and said out loud, "Truth!" I quickly glanced over at my sleeping husband, certain that I had awakened him. He was still asleep, but I wondered how he slept, I had said the word *truth* so loud.

"Father," I whispered into the darkness, "You are the way, the *truth*, and the life. You *are* Truth. I must listen to You. I must believe what You say about me because that is truth."

Don't underestimate the lies from Satan. He whispers strong words of defeat, despair, discouragement, and disillusionment.

He does not want you to believe what Jesus knows and believes about you. Revelation 12:10 says that Satan goes before God and accuses us day and night. Yet in John 8:44, we are told that he is the "father of lies."

That's why when you go through a hard time, Satan takes advantage of your thoughts. If you lose your job, you may think to yourself, *I must not be competent. I'm embarrassed to tell people I got fired. Who will want to hire me now?* Or if you have a child who did not turn out as you had hoped, you may blame yourself and think, *I was a bad parent. I wonder what others are saying behind my back?* Why do we find it so easy to believe the lies from Satan, our accuser, instead of the truth from our loving heavenly Father—in whom there is not one speck of deceit? Oh, how Satan loves to see if he can keep us feeling ineffective.

In addition to Satan taking advantage of the hurtful situations in our lives, I think I've discovered one of the places that Satan does his best lying and accusing work. It is when we stand in front of a mirror. Think about this for a moment. If you're standing in front of the mirror and say to yourself, "My hair looks so ugly today," you're usually alone. No one is there to say, "You've got to be kidding; your hair looks great!" Nor does the mirror talk back to you in fairy-tale mode, "You, my dear, are the fairest of them all." No, you make a self-incriminating comment about yourself, and no one is there to refute it. It stays with you. You believe it. You own it.

Now if someone came up to you and said, "Wow, you're having a really bad hair day," you would probably feel irritated and defensive. But when we *tell ourselves* that something is wrong with our appearance (or whatever), it's somehow okay. We end up receiving and believing the accusations.

In his book *Sacred Influence*, Gary Thomas quotes a woman who said, "God thinks of me as a person of value and I need to agree with Him."[1] Now let me ask you two questions. Do you want to agree with God? Or would you rather disagree with Him? I know I don't want to disagree with the Lord. Yet when I choose to believe the lies of Satan about me, sadly I am doing just that. It's as if I'm saying to God, "I know better than You."

So how do we know and discern God's truth about ourselves? Again, we must know God's Word. It is so important to depend on Scripture, not our feelings. I have known this for years, but God keeps bringing it back to me over and over. He illustrated this principle in a startling way for me last year.

I had the privilege of watching our second granddaughter being born. She wasn't breathing during those first few seconds after birth, and her body had a purplish hue. I waited anxiously for her to take her first breath. The room was silent until little Zoe gasped and let out a loud cry. I watched in amazement as her skin color literally turned pink from her head down to her toes. It was as if I actually watched the breath of God flow into her tiny body.

Standing in that delivery room, I heard the whispers of my heavenly Father: *Marilyn, you saw My breath go into little Zoe. My Word is like that too. It is God breathed, and it is My living and active truth. When you are breathing in My Word it brings life to your entire being.*

Not long after Zoe's birth I read Ephesians 2:10. Though I'd first memorized it long ago in vacation Bible school, the words brought new life to me that day: "We are God's workmanship, created by Christ Jesus . . ." I stopped right there. Who made me? Who made you? God! We are actually His workmanship. In the Greek, *workmanship* means masterpiece. So we are God's masterpiece.

While on sabbatical last summer my husband, Paul, two of our grown children, our nephew, and I toured parts of Europe.

One of the places we visited was the Louvre in Paris. We stood in line for what seemed to be hours to see the famed *Mona Lisa.* The lines were long, and the roped-off area in front of the painting was extremely crowded. People would stare at the *Mona Lisa* in silence and finally squeeze off to the side so another person could move up closer and get a better look. Finally, it was my turn to see the masterpiece. I had seen lots of copies, but this was my first time seeing the real thing. This was the original! If I moved a little, the eyes in the portrait seemed to follow me. We read on a museum pamphlet that no one has been able to reproduce the *Mona Lisa.*

So this is what it means, I mused, *to be God's workmanship—a masterpiece, one of a kind, extremely valuable, and not a copy.* We are each an original design created by Jesus Christ. There is no one else like you or me. And on top of being a masterpiece, we were made in the image of God. We must never forget this.

Not long after we returned home from Europe, Erik Rees, a pastor at Saddleback Church, spoke at our church and mentioned the *Mona Lisa.* "Why is it that so often we want to go around being copies of someone else instead of being the original God made us to be?" he asked. His question hit hard! It would be easy for me to look at another pastor's wife and say, "I wish I could teach or counsel like she does." Or a teen might look at a peer and say, "I wish I had their grades or their popularity with the opposite sex." Or a man in the workplace might think, *I wish I was like my coworker who knows how to network and make the big sales.* We compare, compare, and compare some more with others. Why do we think we will get better by looking at the strengths of others? The fact is, you are God's masterpiece, and as Erik Rees says, "Only you can be you!"[2] Did you get that? *Only you can be you!*

The verse in Ephesians goes on to say that, not only are we

God's masterpieces created by Jesus Christ, but we were "created
. . . to do good works, which God prepared in advance for us to
do." In other words, God is concerned about both our being
and our doing. (I'm so glad He mentions this, because sometimes I still get hung up on performance.) Actually, it's *His* doing
in our lives; we live out doing the things God planned long ago
for us to do. Only *you* can do the good works that He prepared
for you to do before you were born. That is so reassuring! It
means that there are specific things God wants you to do. The
fact that you are breathing right at this moment means God isn't
through with you on earth yet. His plans for you continue—
plans that He has prepared *in advance*.

We don't have to be worried about our performance (or
"doing") either, Ephesians 2:10 assures us. If we are listening
to the Lord and taking one day at a time, He will bring us the
work He designed for us. I believe Jesus wants us to catch the
fact that as we work on our "being" (to know Him and who we
are in Him more fully), we will naturally be productive in our
"doing." And that "doing," whatever it is, will fit us, and we will
feel useful and fulfilled. It may not be noteworthy by the world's
standards, but we will be accomplishing God's Kingdom work,
and there is nothing greater. Jesus told us that His Kingdom
is within us. That means the King is in us, too, helping us to
accomplish the plans and good works He's destined for us to do.

Even though I know the truth of Ephesians 2:10, I must
admit that I still slip up. This past summer I walked down our
driveway to get the newspaper and mail. When I reached the
mailbox I checked to see if the mail had arrived. It hadn't, so I
went back into the house. All of a sudden I remembered that
I didn't pick up the newspaper by the mailbox. I immediately
asked myself, *How could you forget the paper? You were right there.*

A while later I walked back down to the mailbox. This time

163

the mail had arrived. I skimmed through it as I walked back to
the house. The minute I got inside, however, I realized I had forgotten the newspaper again. This time I started to berate myself.
*What is the matter with you? How could you forget the paper two times
in a row? Are you going senile?*

Again, I walked back outside and headed to the mailbox.
Only this time I wasn't just saying these things to myself; I was
actually voicing my negative self-talk out loud. I didn't care if
the neighbors heard me; I was so disgusted with forgetting that
crazy newspaper again.

Marilyn, you are so dumb! Are you losing your mind? On and on I
went until halfway down the driveway. I stopped in my tracks—
both with my words and my feet.

Someone was standing at my mailbox. It may sound crazy, but
I saw what looked like Jesus standing next to my mailbox listening to me as I berated myself. I saw His sad eyes as He looked at
me. I snapped my mouth shut immediately. I could not verbally
bad-mouth myself while looking at Him! No words would
come out of my mouth . . . nor did I want them to.

For the first time I realized how negative self-talk hurts our
Lord Jesus—deeply. When we allow shame and negative self-talk
to dominate our speech and thoughts, we are actually telling the
Lord that His workmanship is defective. We are saying that we
are irregular, seconds, defective, and discounted people—just like
pieces of cast-off clothing. We are not. Jesus doesn't make people
like that. He makes us into brand-new people. His followers
have been bought, *as is*, purchased by the blood of Jesus Christ.

After I got the newspaper I went inside my house and wept
before the Lord. I was led to the passage in Luke 22:54-62
where Peter, a disciple of Jesus, denied that he knew the Lord
even though he had just spent three years with Him. The verse
that caught my heart was the one right after Peter denied Jesus

and the rooster crowed. "The Lord turned and looked straight at Peter" (v. 61). I felt as if I'd seen that same penetrating look as the Lord looked straight at me from beside the mailbox. I realized that, in a sense, I was also denying the Lord.

We deny Jesus every time we disregard His truth and put ourselves down. That hurts us. We deny Him every time we fail to see our value in Him. That hurts us. We deny Him every time we continue to hang on to our self-condemning thoughts and lies. That hurts us too. And then, it's as if Jesus turns and looks straight at us with His eyes of love and compassion, and something dawns on us. We have, in a sense, denied our Lord Jesus, and I wonder if that hurts Him.

That mailbox incident made me pay attention to my self-talk and jerked me back to reality. *So, Father,* I prayed, *show me what to do. How do I allow You, the Spirit of Truth, to penetrate my life and make a difference to break the lie cycle and eradicate the shame language?*

HOW ABOUT YOU?

1. Now that you've been introduced to the shame language, would you say you ever speak it? Have you ever recognized it in the speech of others? If so, how might you lovingly confront yourself or another person speaking it?

2. Can you see areas in your life where Satan has stolen your identity in Christ?

3. Look at the following verses: John 14:16-17; John 15:26; and John 16:13. They all speak of the Spirit of _____. (In other words, truth isn't just a good character trait to possess; Truth is a living person.) How does recognizing this give you hope?

4. Have you ever condemned yourself? Explain. Scripture says, "There is now no condemnation for those who are in Christ Jesus" (Romans 8:1). How would your life be different if you really accepted this truth?

5. Someone once told me, "Shame is responsible for many of the things I can't stand about myself." Can you trace any of the things you can't stand about yourself back to toxic shame?

6. Take some time and write out any lies you believe about yourself.

7. What can you do to begin counteracting these lies?

8. If you wrote down a lie or lies after question 6, seek to find a verse (or verses) that you believe corresponds to your lie(s). Ask the Lord to show you a verse that will help you. You might check

a concordance at the back of your Bible for ideas. For example, if you lack confidence and tell yourself you'll never be good at anything, you could look up the word *confidence*. Commit the verse that counteracts your lie to memory.

9. Put your name in the blanks in the following verse:"For _____ [is] God's workmanship, created in Christ Jesus to do good works, which God prepared in advance for _____ to do" (Ephesians 2:10). What does this Scripture mean to you?

10. Have you allowed yourself to grasp how much God treasures you? Scripture says you are:
   Deeply loved by God
   Completely forgiven and fully pleasing to God
   Totally accepted by God
   A new creation, complete in Christ[3]

   Which phrase above means the most to you? Why?

✻　✻　SHAME *Lifters*　✻　✻

- Daily tell yourself, out loud, that you are royalty! You are a child of the King! Attach this statement to an action you do daily. Perhaps you can voice this affirmation when you are brushing your teeth or putting your keys in the ignition.

Claim your identity even if you don't believe it . . . eventually
you will.

- If you have trouble believing God loves you, begin thanking
  Him by saying, "Father, thank You that You love me!" Instead
  of praying only, "Father, I love You," also learn to say "Father,
  thank You for loving me." It will remind you of two important
  truths: (1) You don't have to try to earn His love, and (2) God
  loved you *first*.

Dear heavenly Father,

Thank You that Your Word says I am no longer under condemnation
(Romans 8:1). Please remind me of this whenever I start to condemn
myself. I do not have the right to condemn myself because Jesus took
my "condemnation papers" from me and paid for them.

Thank You that Your evaluation of me is not based on my perfor-
mance or my feelings. You see me exactly as I am and You love me.

I praise You that You are Truth (John 14:6). You have never lied
and You never will. You are true to Your holy character and to Your
promises. There is no deceit in You (1 Peter 2:22).

Help me to hear Your voice cheering me on instead of the booing of
my enemy. Your words are living, active, God-breathed, and penetrating
(Hebrews 4:12). They give life to my soul.

Thank You that I am one of Your masterpieces, and that You are
pleased with Your creation (Ephesians 2:10). I am not trash. You made
me for You, and that makes me delightfully Yours. In Your name, the
Spirit of Truth, Amen.

ELEVEN

Set Free

So often times it happens that we live our lives in chains
And we never even know we have the key.

— The Eagles, "Already Gone"

The incident at my mailbox showed me how frequently I still put myself down and how it grieved God's heart. That awareness made me stop and think, but I wasn't sure what to do at first. I likened it to driving to a distant place and then accidentally locking the keys in the car. You get a sinking feeling as you look through the car window and see your keys lying on the seat. It's so frustrating to be able to see the keys but not be able to get them. Quickly your mind assesses your situation, trying to come up with different options to unlock the car. Then you realize— you're stuck!

But wait. You remember that there is a little magnetic box holding a spare key somewhere underneath your car frame. You search around with your fingers until you locate the little box. You open it, and there to your relief and joy you have the key. You are no longer locked out.

In the same way, it was as if I could see the key to breaking the shame cycle through the window of my heart. Oh, if I could only reach it! Shame, however, made me feel locked out with no options.

But wait. What a relief to realize that, while I could not unlock the door to self-acceptance on my own, there *was* a spare key—a key that was near and accessible. This key gave me access to the person God intended for me to be. I could be free! Free from self-consciousness. Free from bitterness. Free from regret and guilt. Free from that repetitive voice in my head telling me how worthless I was. I could be free from shame. This master key fit many locks. It opened the door to God, His presence, and His Word. It opened the door of forgiveness. And it gave access to people to come into my life and extend grace to me as I shared my story.

Here is the process (or key) that I discovered as God helped me unlock the chains of shame and untruth in my life. You also can use this key every time you sense that shame is locking you out of peace and joy:

1. Ask the Lord if there is a lie in your life that you believe. Ask Him to reveal any untruths or secrets you may have stashed away. It may take you a while before a lie is unlocked, but I believe the Lord often reveals a lie immediately. He will convict you in areas of untruth that need to be confessed. Do you know what *convict* means? It means to *convince*. The Lord Jesus wants you to recognize and be *convinced* of any untruths that are holding you back. Both John 14:17 and John 16:13 identify the Holy Spirit as the "Spirit of truth." Truth is not just a great word; truth is a *Person*.

2. Admit these untruths, lies, or secrets first to yourself and then confess them to the Lord. Write down any lies the Spirit of truth brings to your mind. Once your eyes have been opened to a lie, confess it. (*Confess* means that you agree with what the Lord has revealed to you.) After you have done that, share what you have discovered with people

you trust. A godly, professional counselor can be very instrumental in your journey of healing, since he or she can offer helpful insights and empathy. Often I've found counselors to be very skilled in asking the right questions to help uncover known and unknown lies. Also, talking with a small group of trustworthy people can provide a safety net of grace for you. It is so important to be able to tell your story to people who won't put you down or try to fix you.

3. Replace all the lies you have believed about yourself with Scripture. Seek to find a verse that corresponds to each lie you've believed and write it down. Even though you may feel the chains of untruth, the Bible says in 2 Timothy 2:9 that "God's word is not chained." It is free to do its powerful work in your life.

But there is a catch. This may sound strange, but when I first realized the lies I believed about myself I wanted to hang on to them. Why? They had been my safe way of relating to others. Let me illustrate with an example of the "I am inadequate" lie. Years ago people who attended my seminars on listening to God began suggesting that I write a book on this topic. My immediate response was, "Oh, I can't do that; I'm not qualified."

They would quickly reassure me, saying, "You're not inadequate; you can do it." I got their affirmation in a roundabout way, which actually encouraged me to hold on to the lie. Why? I got affirmed. More importantly, though, as long as I lived according to that untruth, I didn't have to try anything new. I didn't have to risk. I didn't have to change. I was safe.

Here is an example of the way this lie of inadequacy played out for me when a publisher approached me about writing my first book.

The lie: I am inadequate.

What I believed about this lie: I don't think I'll try to do this project because I'm not qualified. I really can't write—so just to be safe, I'll do nothing. If I don't attempt to write a book, I won't get a rejection slip from the publisher.

God's truth: "I can do everything through him [Christ] who gives me strength" (Philippians 4:13).

Now what was I supposed to do with this truth from Scripture? When the Holy Spirit brought that verse to my attention, I knew I needed to make a choice. Either I was going to believe the truth that Christ would help me do everything, or I would refuse to acknowledge that truth so I could stay in my comfort zone. It was up to me. The Lord also reminded me that when the apostle Paul wrote that verse he was in prison. Talk about having a good reason for feeling inadequate! In the end, this passage helped convince me to send the publisher sample chapters, which led ultimately to the release of my first book, *Listening for God*.

As I began to admit other untruths I believed about myself, I realized Scripture was full of truths to set me free from every one of my negative beliefs. But I'll be honest, believing and owning truth is hard work. You'll want to fall back on your old lies because they are familiar to you. Some of the lies you believe may have been words that were carelessly spoken by people who thought their comments were innocuous. The fact is, over time, their words have had a huge impact on you. And it's hard to disown these words. Yet these untruths of the past are poisoning your present.

There is, however, good news. When the Holy Spirit shows you a verse from Scripture that corresponds to a lie you believe, it has a powerful effect. You know when it is the Holy Spirit speaking to you because His words have power in them. It's as if, when you read a verse, you feel you are looking at your soul in a mirror for the very first time. You hear the verse, you see how it reflects and addresses a soul need, and you exclaim, "Yes! This has my name on it!"

4. Be aware that the lie will come back to you again and again like a CD set on the repeat mode. Whenever the lie returns (and it will)—hit *the "off" button*! Refuse to listen to the accusing voice. I still fall into destructive thought patterns occasionally, but now I recognize them. So when the enemy speaks against me, I am in a position to recognize and deal with his darts much more quickly. I know I have a Savior with a master key to my soul, which fills me with confidence and hope.

One evening my eighteen-year-old son, Paul, asked to borrow my car. I gave him permission, and he spent the evening with his friends. When I got into the car the next morning and started the engine, I almost jumped out of my seat. As soon as I turned on the ignition, his CD blasted out of the car stereo speakers. It was really cranked up! It was so loud it hurt my ears. Immediately, as a knee-jerk reaction, I hit the radio "off" button. Silence. It felt so good not to hear that jarring noise.

Out of the silence, the Lord spoke: *Marilyn, that's what I want you to do whenever you hear the negative accusations, the shame, and the lies from the enemy—hit the off button.* So now, when I hear the enemy whisper my inadequacies to me—*Why did you do that? You're worthless*—I try to recognize the voice as jarring, dissonant noise. I force my mind to stop its racing and I hit the off button immediately. By quoting or searching for a Scripture that corresponds to that inadequacy, it helps to bring silence to my internal warfare. Rather than talking to Satan and telling him to leave me alone (he doesn't deserve any communication from me), I turn my mind toward Scripture.

It does work to hit the off button. But you must be intentional about it, and you must practice turning it off. It does not work to argue with the lies from the enemy, just as it would have been useless for me to have sat in the car trying to convince the CD to be quiet. Our enemy is ruthless, loud, and persistent, and you will not win by arguing.

5. Look into the face of Jesus. Picture Christ. Can you see His face? Can you see His smile? Can you imagine Him holding you? Know that Jesus really is there for you. There is no condemnation of you on His part. He longs to whisper His loving thoughts to you. Fix your eyes on Jesus. Remember: "Those who look to [God] are radiant; their faces are never covered with shame" (Psalm 34:5). Also, "Your love is ever before me, and I walk continually in your truth" (Psalm 26:3).

It is so important to look and listen for the voice of the One who cheers you on—Jesus. Oh, how He longs to communicate with you through His Word and through His quiet whispers as you are still before Him.

In the beginning of this book, I wrote about holding a difficult secret inside. It was a secret that did not birth a good kind of shame but the toxic kind. Now as I finish telling my story, I want to share another secret. A good secret. It is about the secret place of the Most High God mentioned in Psalm 91. Not everybody knows about this place, but, oh, I pray the word spreads. The secret place is available to all who desire it. It is a place of rest in the shadow of our almighty God. It is a place where He draws you to Himself and covers you with His feathers. He tucks you under His wings and offers refuge from all that seeks to steal your peace. It is a place to go deep into the down of His soft, protective feathers and to be safe. It is a place to rest in God's truth and present your newly unlocked soul to the Lord, saying, "Here I am, Jesus. May I find my rest in You this very moment."

Not too long ago I got a fresh illustration of how God longs to speak to us in that secret place. My husband and I had been invited by our friends Craig and Emilie to join them and eleven other married couples at a private hunting lodge. The purpose was simply to relax and enjoy each other's company. There were no speaking seminars; it was just a time of restoration.

Some high-profile people from the Christian community had been invited, so I was a little unsure of myself. Included in this group were well-known author and speaker Beth Moore and her husband, Keith.

One snowy, cold afternoon the husbands went pheasant hunting while the wives stayed back in the cozy lodge enjoying the warmth from the fireplace. We were all sitting at a long table talking. Everyone wanted to have an opportunity to get to know Beth Moore and to talk to her about her books, Bible study videos, and how much God had used her to minister in their lives. I was seated at the opposite end of the table from Beth. All of a sudden, Beth looked down the table, pointed a finger, and said to me, "You. I want to talk to you."

Surely she isn't pointing to me, I thought. *She must be pointing to someone on the other side of me.* Quickly I turned my head to the left to see who she was pointing to. But when I looked in that direction, I realized there was no one sitting there. I was at the end of the table. I turned my head back to Beth. She was still looking my way. Gingerly I pointed to myself and asked, "Me?" Beth's answer was, "Yes, I mean you. I want to talk to you." I was so surprised and honored. We got up from the table and went to a quiet spot in the lodge to talk privately. I felt very privileged that Beth had desired to talk to me. Yet there was something the Lord wanted me to learn from that encounter.

Marilyn, He said, *you were flattered to have someone renowned want to speak to you. I, too, say to each of My children daily, "You. I want to talk to you."*

Think of it—the God of the universe wants to talk to us! He makes it possible for us to talk to Him every day. He wants to point out untruths in our lives. He wants to tell us we can come to Him—shame and all. He is approachable. He wants us to know for sure that He loves us and we don't have to go on living our lives trying to *make* Him love us.

I can tell Him if I feel fearful. I don't have to try to work out my fears first and then go talk to Him. I can tell Him when I'm low, and He enables me to draw from His deep reservoir of hope. I can admit to Him when I feel a wave of sadness washing over me, and He helps pull me from the edge of that dark pit of despair. Or I can tell Him when I feel His deep, bubbly joy. I simply talk to Him as my wise and loving friend—a very intimate friend. Can you see that His face is turned toward you? Can you hear His voice saying, "You. I want to talk to *you*"?

How grateful I am to the Lord, who is the extreme opposite of our enemy. I love how He helps us through the journey of shame with His compassionate, kind, and patient ways. He allows us to see how shame can invade and take over our lives, to see how bitterness bites, how lies destroy, and how forgiveness renews.

Jesus took the little girl inside me—the one who was shamed for having needs, the one left on the side of the road, the one who was abused—and He held me tenderly in His arms. He also took me as an adult who was drowning in shame, verbally abusing myself through self-criticism and lies, and He rescued me. No longer do I continue to wound myself. No longer do I allow the lies to poison me. And no longer do I want my past circumstances, lies, or shame to shape me. I long to be shaped by the Lord Jesus.

He is there for you as well, and He calls for you from that secret place. Do you hear Him? "You. I want to talk to *you*," He repeats. He longs to hold you, and He loves you with a love that cannot be quenched. "I'm absolutely convinced that nothing—nothing living or dead, angelic or demonic, today or tomorrow, high or low, thinkable or unthinkable—absolutely *nothing* can get between us and God's love because of the way that Jesus our Master has embraced us" (Romans 8:38-39, *The Message*, italics mine).

By the grace of God, as you work at eradicating shame in your own life, you can become a shame lifter for others. Share your story. Then listen to people. Really listen to them. Be a godly sounding board, someone who gently points out shame-based statements when you hear them spoken, and when appropriate offers words of truth from Scripture.

Just recently I told my story to a group of women. A woman in her sixties quietly approached me at the end of the session. With a hesitant voice and tears in her eyes she whispered, "I've never told anyone this before, but I was sexually abused as a child by a relative. I've carried this burden all of my life. It is such a relief to finally be able to tell someone." There was pain in this woman's eyes, but there was also a kind of power behind them. It was as if the Holy Spirit had just placed a key in her hand and she was, for the very first time, desiring for that lock to be opened so that she could deal with her shame.

Whether you have been shamed by verbal comments, painful circumstances, or physical, emotional, or sexual abuse, you do not need to walk around with those heavy, dragging chains. There is no shame for those who look to God for help. And when people look at you they will see that your face is clear and open—in fact, it's radiant. The shame on you is gone. Your shame has been removed—moved to the Cross forever.

At the beginning of my journey with God, the day my mother died, I had gone tentatively to the God of my mother. In a childlike way I had asked God to "be a mother to me." A mother's love was the only kind of love I understood. It dawned on me as I finished this chapter that I no longer need God to be solely a mother to me. He has become a Father to me. When did that happen? I finally understood that it all goes back to the key of forgiveness. The day I forgave my dad for not being there for me was a transition day. That was the day God was able to fully become a Father to me. Forgiveness was a huge key. It was being offered to me all the time; I just had to use it.

Recently while driving to a hair appointment, I saw the three boys who live around the corner from us: Matthew, Simeon, and Gabriel. They had just gotten off the school bus at the end of their street, where their father had been waiting for them. I slowed down as I watched the following scenario play out. When his sons reached him, the dad smiled, jostled their hair, and put his arm around each of his son's shoulders to welcome them back from school. They were all smiling, laughing, and talking to one another. At one point, their father threw back his head and laughed when one of his sons told him something humorous.

As I drove away, I saw the father walking with his three boys toward their home. His arm was draped around Gabriel, his youngest son. What a tender scene. It was so Jesus-like. My eyes immediately filled with tears and I had to blink them away so I could see the road as I drove.

I wish I had a father like that, I thought, sighing to myself.

You do, came a soft reply nearby. *I am the Father who waits for you every day. I wait for you to come home. I won't ever forget you. I'll be there to meet you. I will not abandon you. I do not treat you as your sins deserve. I am compassionate and gracious, slow to anger, abounding in love. I desire to be with you, and I always want to talk to you.*

When I returned home later that day, I wrote down what I'd seen. Shortly after that I saw the following verse in my quiet time with the Lord:

> I will be a Father to you, and you will be my sons and daughters, says the Lord Almighty. (2 Corinthians 6:18)

I am a child of the ultimate Shame Lifter, the Lord God Almighty. The shame on me is gone.

HOW ABOUT YOU?

1. Can you name one or more people of grace in your life with whom you can share your deepest self without feeling overexposed or embarrassed?

2. "An honest answer is like a kiss on the lips" (Proverbs 24:26). What does this verse say to you?

3. If you believe a lie about yourself, what makes you want to hold on to it? How might it create a false sense of safety?

4. Second Corinthians 10:5 reminds us to "take captive every thought to make it obedient to Christ." Think of a lie about yourself that you have accepted. Now picture yourself capturing that lie in your hands and giving it to the Lord Jesus. How would your self-talk change if you took this verse to heart?

5. "How strengthening it is, to know that [Jesus] is at this moment feeling and exercising the same love and grace toward me as when He died upon the cross for me," notes John Darby.[1] Can you picture Jesus responding to you that way today? How might this image of Christ's love aid in eliminating your shame?

6. The Lord views you as His child, worthy of His time and love. Your worth matters to Him. He longs for you to live a life that is free from shame and lies. His truth does set you free. Can you visualize His nail-scarred hands reaching out to embrace you? Can you picture yourself being held by Jesus? How does knowing that God longs to connect with you so closely affect how you think about yourself—and Him?

SHAME *Lifters*

- Begin practicing hitting the off button whenever self-condemning thoughts come to your mind. For example, if you catch yourself saying, "I'm so dumb," stop and say, "No, that's a lie! God made me and blessed me with a wonderful mind." To help solidify this habit, at the end of the day take a moment to record in a journal what happened as you refused to dwell on a negative thought.

- I appreciate what a group of twenty courageous women, all from the same church, told me they did recently. They gathered in a circle and invited the Holy Spirit to search their hearts. Each woman then shared a negative thought (lie) she believed about herself. It was the first time many had verbalized their self-criticism out loud. After a woman admitted the lie she believed about herself, the other women in the group were able to come alongside to help refute that person's lie and replace it with God's truth. The women said it was amazing how the Holy Spirit and the body of Christ worked together to help bring them truth and freedom. Would you be willing to take a similar risk with a group of trusted friends? You could end up being shame lifters to one another.

- Look at the cover of this book. Picture yourself blowing away the seeds of your own shame. Watch them leave. Watch how God lifts your shame. You are free.

- My oldest daughter, Christy, and her husband, Adam, pastor an inner-city church. On a particularly crisp morning last fall, my daughter noticed a woman prostitute pacing near their church. She invited her in for coffee and snacks. The woman was hesitant and said, "I'm not really the church-going type."

    Christy said, "That's okay! Just come in for some snacks."

    Over a cup of coffee the woman asked Christy, "Do you know what I do for a living?"

"Yes," my daughter replied.

"And you still invited me in?" the prostitute asked, surprised.

"Yes," Christy affirmed as she continued talking with her.

A few months later the prostitute was jailed for drug possession. Christy visited her in jail and also brought her a book. The woman wrote Christy and Adam a thank-you note after her visit. *"Thank you for seeing more worth in me than I see in myself."*

Being a shame lifter means helping a person (no matter who they are or what their age) to see that they have value and worth. How can you reach out to someone battling shame?

- Now picture the Lord Jesus reaching out to *you* in your shame. He opens the door of *His* heart and knocks on the door of *your* heart. He asks you, "It's cold outside; may I come in?"

"Oh, Jesus, how can You ask to come to me? Do You know what I do? Do You know what I've done?"

"Yes, My child, I know all about you."

"And You still want to be with me?"

"Yes. I want you no matter what you've done or not done. I want you no matter what you think of yourself and why you think you're not worthy. I want you because I long for you to be freed from the heaviness of shame. I want you to feel light again and to experience My joy. I've lifted your shame from you and you don't have to carry it any longer. My child, I am *your* Shame Lifter."

Can you accept His invitation?

Dear heavenly Father,
Thank You that You see me for who I truly am. What do You see when You look inside my life, Father? (Proverbs 20:27). Do You see

any chains that hinder me? Is there something I need to be made aware of?

Please help me to understand and discern Your truth about my situation. Help me to have a sane estimate of myself (Romans 12:3, PHILLIPS). Your Word says You are the "Spirit of truth" (John 15:26). Rouse me from my sleep and help me see if there are any places where my mind, will, or emotions are being held captive with untruth by the evil one. Help me to use the key that You have provided (John 8:32, 36).

Thank You for continuing to love me, even though many times I do not love myself. Help me to stop living my life to try to get You to love me; You already do (1 John 3:1). May I go often to your secret dwelling place to find peace and truth and rest.

Thank You for putting Your arm around me and whispering Your words of truth as You walk me toward home. You remind me once again that You are my Shame Lifter (Hebrews 12:2-3). In the name of the One who is Truth—Jesus—Amen.

FATHER'S LOVE LETTER

My Child . . .

You may not know me, but I know everything about you
. . . *Psalm 139:1*

I know when you sit down and when you rise up
. . . *Psalm 139:2*

I am familiar with all your ways
. . . *Psalm 139:3*

Even the very hairs on your head are numbered
. . . *Matthew 10:29-31*

For you were made in my image
. . . *Genesis 1:27*

In me you live and move and have your being
. . . *Acts 17:28*

For you are my offspring
. . . *Acts 17:28*

I knew you even before you were conceived
. . . *Jeremiah 1:4-5*

I chose you when I planned creation
. . . *Ephesians 1:11-12*

You were not a mistake, for all your days are written in my book
. . . *Psalm 139:15-16*

I determined the exact time of your birth and where you would live
. . . Acts 17:26

You are fearfully and wonderfully made
. . . Psalm 139:14

I knit you together in your mother's womb
. . . Psalm 139:13

And brought you forth on the day you were born
. . . Psalm 71:6

I have been misrepresented by those who don't know me
. . . John 8:41-44

I am not distant and angry, but am the complete expression of love
. . . 1 John 4:16

And it is my desire to lavish my love on you
. . . 1 John 3:1

Simply because you are my child and I am your Father
. . . 1 John 3:1

I offer you more than your earthly father ever could
. . . Matthew 7:11

For I am the perfect father
. . . Matthew 5:48

If you seek me with all your heart, you will find me
. . . Deuteronomy 4:29

Delight in me and I will give you the desires of your heart
. . . Psalm 37:4

For it is I who gave you those desires
... *Philippians 2:13*

I am able to do more for you than you could possibly imagine
... *Ephesians 3:20*

For I am your greatest encourager
... *2 Thessalonians 2:16-17*

I am also the Father who comforts you in all your troubles
... *2 Corinthians 1:3-4*

When you are broken-hearted, I am close to you
... *Psalm 34:18*

As a shepherd carries a lamb, I have carried you close to my heart
... *Isaiah 40:11*

One day I will wipe away every tear from your eyes
... *Revelation 21:3-4*

And I'll take away all the pain you have suffered on this earth
... *Revelation 21:3-4*

I am your Father, and I love you even as I love my son, Jesus
... *John 17:23*

For in Jesus, my love for you is revealed
... *John 17:26*

He is the exact representation of my being
... *Hebrews 1:3*

He came to demonstrate that I am for you, not against you
... *Romans 8:31*

And to tell you that I am not counting your sins
... *2 Corinthians 5:18-19*

Jesus died so that you and I could be reconciled
... *2 Corinthians 5:18-19*

His death was the ultimate expression of my love for you
... *1 John 4:10*

I gave up everything I loved that I might gain your love
... *Romans 8:31-32*

If you receive the gift of my son Jesus, you receive me
... *1 John 2:23*

And nothing will ever separate you from my love again
... *Romans 8:38-39*

Come home and I'll throw the biggest party heaven has
ever seen
... *Luke 15:7*

I have always been Father, and will always be Father
... *Ephesians 3:14-15*

My question is ... Will you be my child?
... *John 1:12-13*

I am waiting for you
... *Luke 15:11-32*

*Love, your Dad, Almighty God**

---

* Father's Love Letter used by permission of Father Heart Communications, copyright ©
1999–2008, www.FathersLoveLetter.com.

APPENDIX A: Recognizing a Shame Giver

Self-absorbed
Abusive
Hostile
Indifferent
Uninvolved
Critical
Punishes harshly
Speaks truth without grace
Uses the word *should* frequently
Tears you down in private and in group settings
Makes you feel exposed
Interrupts
Doesn't believe in you or your dreams
Uses "you" statements (e.g., "You should have known better.")
Invalidates you through his or her body language (e.g., rolls eyes, glares, covers ears, points finger)
Uses sarcasm
Shames you for having needs
Compares you to others
Embarrasses you
Jokes at your expense
Seeks to control you
Uses a negative "parent" voice
Mimics your voice or behavior
Oversteps your boundaries
Makes you feel invisible
Holds grudges
Reminds you that you are worthless
Communicates that you are not good enough, inadequate, a pain

APPENDIX B: Recognizing a Shame Lifter

Careful when disciplining
Shares truth bathed in grace
Suggests what you might want to do, not what you "should" do
Builds you up in private and in public settings
Covers and protects you
Listens without interrupting
Believes in you and dreams with you
Uses "I" statements
Encourages
Refrains from negative facial or hand expressions
Recognizes that sarcasm is a form of inner anger
Recognizes your needs and asks to help
Will not tell you someone is better than you
Makes you look good in front of others
Says only the best about you and does not divulge secrets
Lets you be you without controlling you
Talks to you on a "peer" level instead of talking down to you
Does not make fun of your words or actions
Puts up safe boundaries
Sees and notices you
Forgives you and does not bring up your transgression again
Reminds you that you are royalty of the King
Communicates that you are loved, valued, treasured—the best!

APPENDIX C: Recognizing a Shame Receiver

Apologizes profusely even when something isn't his or her fault
Extreme people pleaser, overachiever
Feels responsible for everything
Denies needs
Perfectionist—always tries to do the right thing
Fails to meet his or her own expectations
Blames someone else if something doesn't go right
Tends to procrastinate
Difficulty hearing and receiving affirmation
Puts *himself* or *herself* down
Puts *others* down because he or she dislikes self
Believes he or she is defective
Deals with daily self-rejection
Continually notices his or her own faults and flaws even though
    no one else does
Believes he or she has nothing to offer and consequently sabo-
    tages his or her own success
Timid body language: looks away from others, slumps shoulders,
    stammers, etc.
Easily embarrassed
Wishes he or she could evaporate or disappear
Finds it easy to withdraw
Finds it difficult to dream or wish for something
Self-criticism is so heavy inside he or she cannot accept more
    criticism from the outside
Criticizes self before others can
Believes thoughts that he or she is worthless, unwanted, weak,
    dirty, incompetent

Seeks to be in control because inwardly he or she feels out of control

Denies his or her true feelings

Monitors and guards what he or she says—may also speak softly or in whispers

Feels empty

Feels something is wrong with him or her

May wrestle with eating disorders

Often struggles with addictions

Prone to lying—whether to others or self

APPENDIX D: Shame-Based Self-Talk

Common Lies People Believe about Themselves

I am ...
Unworthy
Stupid
Ugly
Fat
Boring
Bad
Uninteresting
Inadequate
An airhead
A mistake
A nothing
A bad friend
Obnoxious
Useless
A loser

I am no one.
I'm not worthy of friendship.
I am nothing but a failure.
I'm too old to be of much importance anymore.
I'm a "has been."
I can't do anything right.
I will fail.
I have no value.
If I talk, people will know I'm not smart.

I'm not a good spouse.
I deserve the hurts life has given me.
Not as good as others
No one would love me if they knew all my secrets.
Can't measure up
Can't believe God would forgive me for what I've done
No one would want me.
There is something wrong with me.

---

* Note: All of these statements come directly from the unofficial surveys I've taken among my speaking audiences.

APPENDIX E: The Shame of Sexual Abuse: A Hidden Epidemic

Sexual abuse is not the cause of all shame, but since acknowledging my own abuse I've come to realize how devastating it is. Sadly, sexual perpetrators treat their victims as objects that can be abused and discarded for the abusers' own pleasure. The following statistics highlight the problem.

One in 4 girls is sexually abused before age 18.

One in 6 boys is sexually abused before age 18.

One in 5 children receive a sexual solicitation while online.

Most victims of sexual abuse never report these incidents.

There are 39 million survivors of childhood sexual abuse in the United States.

More than 67 percent of all sexual assault victims are under age 18.

The median age of sexually abused victims is 9 years old.

One of 7 victims of sexual assault reported to law enforcement agencies is under the age of 6.

Between 30 and 40 percent of victims are abused by family members; another 50 percent are abused by others they know and trust. Fewer than 10 percent of abusers are strangers.

Many victims of child sexual abuse report physical, psychological, and social problems. They also have a higher risk of engaging in risk-taking behaviors such as drugs, alcohol, eating disorders, and suicide and are more likely to be sexually promiscuous than their nonabused peers.

For the sources of these statistics, as well as additional statistics on sexual abuse, see "Statistics Surrounding Child Sexual Abuse" at http://www.darkness2light.org/KnowAbout/statistics_2.asp. Darkness to Light is a national nonprofit organization dedicated to reducing the incidence of child sexual abuse through public awareness and education.

MY PRAYER FOR YOU

Thank you for taking the time to read *Shame Lifter*. As I wrote and prayed over this book, I prayed for you, the reader. I've asked the Lord to use this book to help lead you toward healing or to enable you to come alongside someone who is hurting. I prayed this book would help you see the destructive damage that toxic shame can do. I also prayed that you would be freed from anything that holds you back from becoming all that Jesus has in mind for you. You do not have to stay locked in shame.

Remember that the enemy of your soul, Satan, loves to come and snatch away any seeds of truth the Lord plants in the soil of your heart. I will continue to pray that the seeds He sowed will remain and will produce an abundant harvest of peace and truth.

Victory over shame *is* possible. As I travel around speaking, I hear many stories from other people who are fighting hard to remove their shackles of shame. One that especially touched me came from a young woman whom I first met as a teen. Today Sarah Bokma is a wife, mother of four, and songwriter. Here's her story in her own words:

> When I walked down the aisle as a bride it was anything but a grand day. Our daughter was nearly one, and I was four months pregnant with our son. I was not a pure, beautiful bride, and my heart was broken with shame. I didn't get to shop for the wedding dress of my dreams; instead my dress was made from ivory yellow fabric. As I walked down the aisle on my dad's arm, I felt embarrassed, judged, and so ashamed I wanted to cry rather than rejoice.
>
> I have been married ten years now. They have been years of healing and grieving. I finally understand the bride that I am to Christ—that because of who I am in Him, He now

says to me, "Daughter, put on the white dress of redemption. Wear it with pride—and walk down the aisle of life on your heavenly Daddy's arm. You are pure, you are Mine, beautiful, radiant Bride."

Sarah longs for people to know just how much God treasures them. She wrote the following song as a testimony of the Lord's grace to her. She hopes it might speak to you, or a special woman in your life, as well.

Daughter Wear White
Pure daughter
Nothing in your past can hold you back
You are pure
You are mine
Beautiful, radiant bride
Daughter, wear white.

I have taken off your rags
Removed your shame
Shed all your old ways
You're sheltered by my Name
You are glorious to me
I am enthralled by your beauty
You are free, you are light
Unblemished in my sight.

I have dressed you in light
Robed you to shine
Lifted you from the mire
Displayed you as mine
You are glorious to me

I am enthralled by your beauty
You are free, you are light
You are free, free to shine

All that's been stolen has been returned
All that was lost, redeemed
All I designed you to be you are, My Princess!*

Truly, when we have a breakthrough in our life and are "dressed in his light and robed to shine," our heavenly Father must smile, throw back His head, and laugh with joy for His child. Oh, how He loves you!

"Those who look to him for help will be radiant with joy; no shadow of shame will darken their faces" (Psalm 34:5, NLT).

---

* Words by Sarah Bokma; music by Paula Davis Stitt. Used by permission.

A NOTE TO YOU FROM MARILYN

Part of my journey of healing was to write a fairy tale in which I retell the story of abuse, shame, and restoration in a different genre. Writing this story helped me deal with the fallout from the sexual abuse I experienced as a little girl, and I hope it will be particularly meaningful to others who battle toxic shame as a result of such abuse.

To read this story, "It Happened Once upon a Time," visit the *Shame Lifter* page at http://www.christianbookguides.com.

Let me encourage you to tell or write out your own story as well. You can do so in many ways: for instance, you can talk about it over coffee with a close friend or in the privacy of a counseling session; you can write about it in a journal entry or in a fairy tale, short story, poem, or song lyrics. Telling your story—whether to one person or many people—not only will help you come to terms with your shame, it will let others know they are not alone. Your story will reassure them that others have walked along a similar path and that there is hope.

Whether you are continuing on your journey to rise above shame or are in a place where you can help others who are hurting, I would enjoy hearing from you. While I am not qualified to give professional counsel, I do welcome your thoughts and comments. Please feel free to contact me at the following address:

Marilyn Hontz
c/o Author Relations
Tyndale House Publishers
351 Executive Drive
Carol Stream, IL 60188

ENDNOTES

Introduction

1. John Bradshaw, *Healing the Shame That Binds You* (Deerfield Beach, FL: Health Communication, 1988), 10.
2. Advocates for Survivors of Child Abuse, "Dealing with Shame and Blame," http://www.asca.org.au/survivors/survivors_shame.html.
3. Stephen Seamands, *Wounds That Heal* (Downers Grove, IL: InterVarsity Press, 2003), 44.
4. Robert S. Vibert, "Avoiding Responsibilities in Life," http://www.shiftinaction.com/node/2050.

Chapter Two: Loved like Crazy

1. Robert Brooks and Sam Goldstein, *Raising Resilient Children* (New York: McGraw-Hill, 2001), 11.

Chapter Four: Neglected

1. Rick Richardson, *Experiencing Healing Prayer* (Downers Grove, IL: InterVarsity Press, 2005), 123.

Chapter Five: Loss after Loss

1. "Leaving on a Jet Plane," words and music by John Denver, 1967.
2. William E. Mann, ed., *Augustine's Confessions: Critical Essays* (Lanham, MD: Rowman and Littlefield, 2006), 108. This is found in Augustine's *Confessions* IX, 12.

Chapter Six: My Other Father

1. The Institute is now known as Jerusalem University College.
2. If you'd like to read more about how to hear God speak to you, see my book *Listening for God* (Carol Stream, IL: Tyndale, 2004).

Chapter Seven: Seeing the "Give" in Forgiveness

1. Sandra Wilson, *Hurt People Hurt People* (Grand Rapids, MI: Discovery House, 2001).
2. C. H. Spurgeon quote taken from Nancy Leigh DeMoss, *Choosing Forgiveness* (Chicago: Moody, 2006), 18.

Chapter Eight: Forgive and Reforgive

1. Karl Barth, *Prayer*, ed. Don Saliers (Louisville, KY: Westminster John Knox Press, 2002), 55.

2. Chuck Lynch, *I Should Forgive But . . .* (Nashville: Word Publishing, 1998), 64–65.
3. Jennifer Kennedy Dean, "The Privilege of Sacrifice," in *Seasons of a Woman's Heart*, ed. Lynn D. Morrissey (Lancaster, PA: Starburst Publishers, 1999), 204.
4. Quoted in Marjorie Rosen, "Winning the Grudge Match," *Ladies Home Journal* (September 2003).
5. Quoted in *Rick Warren's Ministry Toolbox* #251 (March 22, 2006), http://Legacy.pastors.com/RWMT/?ID=251.

Chapter Nine: Intermingling the Good and the Bad
1. Dan B. Allender, *When Trust Is Lost: Healing for Victims of Sexual Abuse* (Grand Rapids, MI: RBC Ministries, 1992), 2. (Emphasis in original.)
2. Ibid., 17.
3. Rick Richardson, *Experiencing Healing Prayer: How God Turns Our Hurts into Wholeness* (Downers Grove, IL: InterVarsity Press, 2005), 159.
4. From chapter 4 of *The Climax of the Risen Life* (Dorset, England: Overcomers Literature Trust, 1900). Quoted in Nick Harrison, *His Victorious Indwelling* (Grand Rapids, MI: Zondervan, 1998), 216–217.
5. Simone Weil, *Gravity and Grace*, trans. Arthur Wills (New York: G. P. Putnam's Sons, 1952), 132.
6. Richardson, *Experiencing Healing Prayer*, 37.

Chapter Ten: Unlearning the Shame Language
1. Gary Thomas, *Sacred Influence* (Grand Rapids, MI: Zondervan, 2006), 14.
2. Erik Rees, "Only You Can Be You," a message given at Central Wesleyan Church in Holland, Michigan, on February 3, 2007.
3. Robert S. McGee, *The Search for Significance* (Nashville: Word Publishing, 1998), 306.

Chapter Eleven: Set Free
1. Quoted by Nick Harrison, *His Victorious Indwelling* (Grand Rapids, MI: Zondervan, 1998), 226.

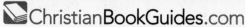

A bonus story
by Marilyn Hontz,

"It Happened
Once upon a Time,"

is available on the *Shame Lifter* page at
http://www.christianbookguides.com.

CP0307

How an ordinary person
can learn to hear God speak

LISTENING *for*
GOD

"Begin to recognize God's whispers
within your own heart."
John C. Maxwell
Founder, The INJOY Group

Marilyn Hontz

God loves you deeply and longs to speak to you. The question is, are you listening?

With refreshing humility and openess, Marilyn Hontz explains how God taught her to reconize his voice and filled her with renewed purpose and an assurance of his unfailing love.

Listening for God will help you get beyond busyness and distractions and enable you to live out ordinary days with the extraordinary power that comes from hearing and listening to God's voice.

A Destiny-Changing
Journey
toward Freedom,
Forgiveness,
and Healthier
Relationships

Healing Your Family Tree

BEVERLY
HUBBLE TAUKE

You can overcome your family's past—and create a new legacy of hope for the future.

*A*re there wounds in your family's history that have never fully healed? Do your family members seem trapped in unhealthy relationship patterns? And do you want something better than this for yourself and your children?

In *Healing Your Family Tree*, family counselor Beverly Hubble Tauke offers eight life-changing principles for family transformation and shares inspiring true stories of families who have overcome hurtful relationship habits. By putting an end to the cycle of negativity, your family members can find the joy that God intended for them and enjoy healthy relationships for generations to come.